BEAUTIFUL

BRIDAL CAKES

THE WILTON WAY

EDITED BY EUGENE T. AND MARILYNN C. SULLIVAN

A word from the president

All of us at Wilton are proud to offer you this beautiful new book. In it you'll find scores of fresh ideas for dazzling wedding cakes, groom's cakes and shower cakes. We've taken special care to make our cake descriptions clear and complete so you'll find it easy to reproduce these master-pieces, or adapt them to your own taste.

For any of the unique pans, and quality tools and ornaments you may need, please check with your local Wilton dealer—or write directly to us. Best wishes!

Vincent A. Naccarato

VINCENT A. NACCARATO

DECORATING CONSULTANT: Norman Wilton

CO-EDITORS:
Marilynn C. and
Eugene T. Sullivan

DECORATORS:
Michael Nitzsche, Senior decorator;
Amy Rohr, Dong Tuy Hoa, and
Dong Quy Nhung.
Contributing decorator, John Walter

ART ASSISTANTS:
Sandra Larson, Joyce Stelcher

EDITORIAL ASSISTANT: Melissa Jess

PRODUCTION ASSISTANT: Ethel LaRoche

READER'S EDITOR: Diane Kish

STAFF PHOTOGRAPHER: Edward Hois

Editorial mail should be addressed to:
  Wilton Book Division
  1603 South Michigan Avenue
  Chicago, Illinois 60616

Library of Congress Cataloging in Publication Data
Main entry under title:

Beautiful Bridal Cakes the Wilton Way.

    1. Cake decorating. I. Sullivan, Eugene T.,
II. Sullivan, Marilynn. III. Wilton Enterprises.
TX771.W53 1978   641.8/653   78-7472
ISBN 0-912696-12-5

BEAUTIFUL BRIDAL CAKES THE WILTON WAY
is published by Wilton Enterprises, Inc.

Dear friends,

This book was created for you—whether you are a decorating novice, learning the fundamentals of the craft, or an accomplished professional.

For each of you, creating a beautiful bridal cake is a dream and a challenge.

These towering, architectural confections are a decorator's delight. The ascending tiers offer a marvelous opportunity for lovely icing embellishments. And no cake contributes more to the pleasure of others than a beautifully trimmed wedding cake. It is the center of all eyes at the reception and becomes a treasured memory for the bride and groom and their families.

So here is a new collection of bridal cakes to inspire you to decorate your own unique masterpieces. Some are quite easy to achieve, others require experience and skill—but we've done our best to make each one beautiful. We've included some outstanding shower cakes and handsome cakes for the groom. For your convenience, all the patterns you'll need are printed in this book.

I'd like to make a request. After you've had the fun of browsing through this book and seeing all the stunning cakes, please read Chapter One carefully. It's really the most important chapter in the book, and I've given a lot of my own time to it. If you're a beginning decorator, it will be the answer to many questions. If you've had a lot of experience, it's a good review of time-tested methods.

I hope you'll enjoy Beautiful Bridal Cakes. We've enjoyed preparing it for you. As always, I appreciate hearing your comments and suggestions.

Sincerely,

Norman Wilton

NORMAN WILTON

BEAUTIFUL BRIDAL CAKES THE WILTON WAY

CHAPTER ONE

How to achieve your beautiful bridal cake...the centerpiece of your wedding

YOUR BEAUTIFUL BRIDAL CAKE is much more than just a cake—it is the striking centerpiece of your wedding reception—and a highlight of the wedding itself. This lovely confection is the symbol of love's promise and should be adorned with all the signs of love—hearts, cupids, flowers, curves and ruffles of icing, fragile lace.

So devote your thoughts, time and devotion to making sure this cake will be a once-in-a-lifetime creation. Years after the last morsel is eaten you will cherish the memory of its beauty.

How to plan your cake

Leaf through this book and others for inspiration. You may find just the design you want—or one that can be modified to achieve the perfect cake for your wedding. Consult with your decorator, baker or caterer for still more ideas. *And be sure to read this chapter* for practical suggestions.

FIRST DETERMINE THE NUMBER OF SERVINGS you will need for the guests at your reception. Since most brides freeze the top tier to serve on the first anniversary, the number of servings for that tier are printed separately. If you are planning a large gathering of 250 or more, look first at the cakes in Chapter Two for ideas. To serve a small, intimate group, turn to page 112. Here are little jewels of cakes that serve 100 guests or much fewer. Consult page 125 for charts that give the number of servings each tier provides. If a design is appealing to you, but the number of servings it provides is too few or too great, the suggestions on the following page will show how the size can be adjusted.

CHOOSE YOUR COLOR SCHEME. Many of today's brides prefer a cake in airy pastels that echo the colors of the bridesmaids' gowns. Others choose classic white, untouched by any tint, or set off with colorful flowers. Some decide on the rich color and flavor of chocolate. (See a handsome example on page 75.)

DECIDE ON TRIM. Piped or gum paste flowers that mimic the ones you will carry are lovely. Icing lace, perhaps a copy of that on the bridal gown, adds a delicate touch. The pictures in this book will prove to you that the decorative possibilities of icing are almost endless.

The choice of ornament gives distinction too. It can be trimmed with the flowers used on the cake for a custom look. You may even have a unique handmade ornament or an entire miniature wedding party! Consult your decorator and pages 19, 31, and 98 for inspiration.

Simplicity is always beautiful

Great Day, on the opposite page, proves that a lovely wedding cake can be decorated quickly. Attractive proportions, lustrous swirls of icing, and a dainty double ring ornament set off the beauty of fresh flowers. This is an easy cake to vary by using icing in a pastel tint and matching the flowers to those used in the bridal bouquet.

PREPARE THE TIERS. You need 8", 12" and 16" round tiers, each two layers. Bake from your favorite recipe, and chill. Use 18", 14" and 10" plates from the Lace Cake Stand and two 7¾" pillars.

ICE AND ASSEMBLE the tiers just as explained on pages 7 and 9. Use the Boiled Icing—Egg White recipe on page 127, stroking it on in decorative swirls. Circle the base of each tier with tube 21 rosettes. Hold the decorating cone perpendicular to tier base, start in center and circle around.

ADORN WITH FRESH FLOWERS. Set ornament on top tier and insert a Flower Spike on either side of it. Insert five spikes in middle tier and six in base tier, following picture for placement. Fill the spikes with water, using an eyedropper, then add flowers. Great Day serves 186, not including the 30-serving top tier.

If you fall in love with a design, but the cake is either too large or too small for your needs, it's usually easy to adjust the size.

INCREASE, OR DECREASE, TIER SIZES. Any cake whose smallest tier measures 8″ or more in diameter may be modified for fewer servings by decreasing the size of each tier by 2″. The tiers of Daffodil, page 41, measure 8″, 12″ and 16″, and omitting the top tier, serve 186. Change the tier sizes to 6″, 10″ and 14″ and serve 140 guests. Reverse this process to achieve a larger number of servings.

SURROUND A CAKE with "satellite" cakes. Any cake built on the Arched Pillars or Lace Cake Stand will look lovely with, or without, surrounding smaller cakes. Prelude and Morning Song on pages 25 and 27 are good examples. Without the four heart cakes, Prelude would serve only 140. Morning Song would serve 186 instead of its present 474 without the six surrounding cakes. Some hostesses like to decorate sheet cakes to "back-up" the wedding cake itself.

ADD, OR SUBTRACT, A TIER. Many designs lend themselves to this modification. Medallion on page 87 serves 116 in its original size. Omit the base tier and it becomes a petite cake serving 50 as you can see in the picture below. Add a 14″ round base tier to Petite Chocolate Rose, page 122, trim with harmonizing loops and roses and it will serve 142 guests instead of 50.

Consult the serving charts on page 125, examine the cake portraits in this book, and you'll usually find whatever design you choose can be made larger or smaller to suit your needs.

Almost any cake mix or recipe is suitable for a bridal cake and the preferences of the bride and groom are given first consideration. See Chapter Seven, page 123, for ideas. If you plan to cover the tiers with rolled fondant, choose a firm applesauce, pound cake, or fruitcake recipe. Foreign method cakes are usually fruitcake (see page 104).

BAKE THE TIERS. Most lower tiers are 4″ high, two layers, so make sure that the baked layers are approximately 2″ high. The small top tier is also two layers, but usually 3″ high, so these baked layers should each be about 1½″ high. See page 125 for approximate amounts of batter—your own experience is the best guide.

NEAT, LEVEL TIERS are necessary for decorating, so follow these tips to achieve them. After batter is poured into pans, lift them a few inches above the table and drop. Now swirl the batter from the center to the sides of the pan. Before baking, pin 2″ strips of damp terry cloth around the outside of the pans. (Tear the strips from an old towel.)

WHEN LAYERS ARE BAKED, cool in pan for ten minutes, run knife around edges and turn out of pan on towel-covered rack. Immediately, put second rack on layer, and turn over to cool completely. Layer will be right side up, with no rack marks.

ALWAYS CHILL OR FREEZE the baked layers on racks before icing. This makes them much easier to handle and allows you to bake them some days ahead of decorating time. *If the layers are still not level*, it is easy to trim them now with a serrated knife. Allow frozen layers to thaw an hour or less before icing.

ATTACH CARDBOARD CAKE CIRCLE, the same size, under every tier before icing. This circle makes it easier to move the tier, easier to separate stacked tiers for serving, and prevents knife scratches on tray or separator plate when the tier is being cut. The next paragraph tells how to move the layer and attach circle.

HOW TO MOVE BOTTOM LAYERS the easy way. Lay wax paper on top of chilled layer, then place a cardboard cake circle, same size or larger, on the wax paper. Put one hand below rack, other on cake circle, and turn over. Remove rack. Put a few dabs of royal icing or thin strokes of corn syrup on the bottom of the layer (now on top). Attach cardboard cake circle, same size as layer. Turn over again and set on turntable to ice. Remove circle and wax paper.

NOTE: *this method also applies to iced tiers.* Just let the icing crust a little before moving.

Here is the Wilton method for icing tiers with either buttercream or boiled icing. Most cakes in this book were iced in buttercream. Recipes are on pages 126 and 127.

PIPE A RING OF ICING around top edge of layer, then spread filling or icing inside ring. Place cake circle on top of chilled top layer, leaving a little of the top uncovered. Turn over as described for bottom layer at left. Rest uncovered portion of upside down top layer on edge of bottom layer and slowly slide cake circle out until top layer rests entirely on bottom layer. Brush crumbs from cake, then brush with apricot glaze (heat apricot jam to boiling and strain) to seal in any other crumbs. Or spread with a thin layer of icing. Dry until a crust forms, about 10 minutes.

COVER CAKE, using long, even strokes. Spread plenty of icing on side with a long spatula, building up edges slightly higher than cake. Work from the bottom up. Mound icing in center of top and spread to blend with edges. Use plenty of icing, covering cake completely and evenly.

SMOOTH TOP using a long metal ruler or piece of stiff cardboard. Pull straight across cake, bringing excess icing toward you. To smooth sides, hold spatula against cake side and slowly spin turntable. If you wish, swirl icing with spatula instead of smoothing it. When icing sets, remove tier to tray, cake board or separator plate.

Proper assembly of a tier cake is the most important step in its creation. Without firm, strong supports, the weight of the upper tiers would crush those below, the cake might shift or even collapse! Please study these two pages carefully—these methods will insure that your masterpiece will stand erect and beautiful at the reception.

Dowel assembly. As a base, use a strong tray, or make a sturdy cake board 2″ larger on each side of the base tier. Use ½″ thick plywood, masonite or four thicknesses of corrugated cardboard. Cover the board with colored foil. (Purchase from a florist or florist supply house.) Cut 4″ larger than the board and tape underneath.

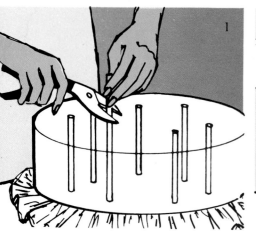

1. First, secure iced base tier to the prepared cake board. (Dab board with stiff royal icing, glucose or corn syrup for "glue".) Using a cardboard cake circle one size smaller than the next tier, center it on the base tier and press it gently into the icing, then remove, to mark an outline. If the second tier is 10″ or less, position seven ¼″ dowel rods within the outline. Use this as a rule: *the larger and more numerous the upper tiers, the more dowels needed.* Really big cakes, like those in Chapter Two, need ½″ dowels in base tier. Push the dowels down into the tier to touch the base, then lift up and clip off the exposed portions with wire cutters or pruning shears. (Use a coping saw for ½″ dowels.) Push the dowels back into the tier until level with the top.

2. Center a clear plastic-wrapped cardboard cake circle, same size as middle tier, on base tier.

Place the tier in position, attaching with royal icing, syrup or glucose. (The plastic will not stick to icing on base tier when middle tier is removed for slicing.) Center a cardboard cake circle one size smaller on top of the middle tier. Press lightly into the icing, then remove to mark an outline. If the next tier or plate is 8″ or less, position five dowel rods within the outline. For larger tiers, follow the rule at left. Push down to cardboard beneath tier, then lift, clip exposed portions and push back into tier so they are level with the surface. To prevent tiers from slipping sideways, sharpen a long ¼″ dowel rod, push through center of both tiers and clip off level with top of middle tier.

3. Position separator plate, with pillars in place, by pushing the pegs supplied with the plate, into the tier until the plate rests on top. When decorating, pipe a trim around edge of plate.

4. Finally, place top tier on its separator plate. Remove cardboard cake circle from under tier first, so the ridges on plate will hold tier securely. Position plate on the pillars. (Page 7 tells how to move an iced tier.)

Tuk-n-ruffle adds a dainty look to a cake. After iced base tier is placed on cake board, push sewn edge of ruffle under cake with a small spatula. Or circle the tier with ruffle and staple in place. Now pipe bottom border on base tier.

OTHER METHODS OF TIER CAKE CONSTRUCTION

ASSEMBLING TIERS
WITH CLEAR DIVIDERS

BUILDING WITH THE LACE CAKE STAND

ASSEMBLING TIERS WITH CLEAR DIVIDERS. This achieves a bridal cake whose tiers seem to float. Lily of the Valley, page 39, is an example.

FILL AND ICE all three tiers—16″, 12″ and 8″ (see page 7). Set the 16″ tier on a serving tray or cake board. Attach with dabs of stiff royal icing, glucose or corn syrup. Set the 12″ tier on a 14″ separator plate, 8″ tier on 10″ separator plate, attaching each in the same way.

FIT THE CLEAR LEGS into the separator plates of the two upper tiers. Hold middle 12″ tier above base tier. Make sure it is centered, then, holding tier by edge of plate, push down until legs touch the cake board beneath base tier.

Hold top tier above middle tier, center, and push into middle tier. NOTE: be sure legs line up.

DECORATE THE ASSEMBLED CAKE, starting with base tier. Or you may remove plates from legs of two top tiers and decorate each tier individually. Always take tiers apart to transport cake, then assemble again at the reception.

MINI-TIER CAKES are constructed the same way.

BUILDING WITH THE LACE CAKE STAND. We are using Great Day, the cake shown on page 4, as an example, but the procedure will be the same for any cake, regardless of the number of tiers.

CUT A HOLE in the center of each corrugated cardboard cake circle needed for the tiers—16″, 12″ and 8″ for Great Day. To position holes, fold paper circles the same size into quarters and snip points. Slip the circles over the lower end of one of the columns to make sure holes are large enough. Place paper circles on cardboard cake circles, mark positions of holes and cut out with a sharp knife. Save the paper circles. Place filled tiers on prepared cake circles and ice the tiers.

USING THE PAPER CIRCLES again, mark the position of hole in center of each lower tier (*not the top tier*). Cut holes in two lower tiers with the Cake Corer.

DECORATE AFTER CAKE IS ASSEMBLED. Place iced 16″ tier on 18″ footed base plate. Insert column and screw to secure. Set 12″ tier on 14″ plate and secure column. Set 10″ plate on column and secure with nut. Set 8″ tier on 10″ plate. Now decorate cake.

OR DECORATE TIER BY TIER. Set 16″ tier on 18″ base plate and decorate. Set 12″ tier on 14″ plate, then set on 12″ cake pan to steady, and decorate. Assemble these two tiers with pillars, add 10″ top plate and secure with nut. Set 8″ tier on top plate and decorate this tier on assembled cake.

9

There are many lovely ways to use piped flowers on a wedding cake as the pages that follow show. Always successful is the classic cascade. Flowers are massed at the edge of the tiers and brought down the sides for a soft rounded look. It's a very quick and easy way to make a cake beautiful.

Any lightweight flower may be used—drop flowers, small wild roses or sweet peas as shown on Spring Beauty opposite page. See the cakes pictured on pages 54, 60 and 119. Pipe them in advance in royal icing. Then the cascades can be made very easily and quickly.

How to decorate Spring Beauty

PIPE THE SWEET PEAS with tubes 103 and 104 in royal icing in two tints of violet. You will need about 225, but these flowers are quick to make.

BAKE THE ROUND TIERS—16″, 12″ and 8″, each two layers. Fill and ice. Set 16″ tier on 20″ cake board. Assemble the two lower tiers using dowels in the base tier as shown on page 8. Set 8″ tier on a 9″ round separator plate, fit with clear pillars and push pillars into middle tier until they touch cardboard cake circle beneath it. (See page 9.)

DECORATE TIERS. Divide 16″ base tier into 16ths. Pipe a tube 18 bottom shell border, then drop a string guideline from mark to mark. Following guidelines, pipe tube 18 zigzag garlands. Add fleurs-de-lis with tube 16 at points of garlands, omitting every fourth one. Pipe tube 16 zigzag garlands on top of tier, lining up with those below.

On side of 12″ tier, mark four hearts with 2½″ cutter. Pipe tube 18 base shell border, then drop guidelines for 16 garlands, using garlands on tier below as guide. Pipe garlands with tube 16, then pipe marked hearts with curving shells using same tube. Add rosettes to points of garlands. Pipe tube 17 reverse shell top border.

Divide top tier into twelfths, drop string guidelines and pipe zigzag garlands with tube 16. Top points of garlands with tube 14 fleurs-de-lis and rosettes. Add tube 16 reverse shell top border.

Trim the cake with flowers

Arrange four cascades of sweet peas on base and middle tiers as explained at right. Add clusters, done in same way, at base of bottom tier. Trim with tube 66 leaves. On top tier attach a sweet pea at base of tier in space between each garland. Pipe tube 66 leaves. Remove artifical flowers from bell of ornament. Pipe icing in bell and press in sweet peas. Set ornament on tier, pipe a mound of icing

at side and arrange assymetrical cascade. Cake serves 186 guests, without 30-serving top tier.

SWEET PEAS are fun to make! Hold tube 104 (or 103) at a 45° angle with wide end of tube on surface. For center petal, squeeze, lift slightly, relax pressure, come back to surface and stop pressure. Set tube to left and right and repeat motions for side petals.

PIPE A DIAMOND SHAPE with point on top of tier, second point on side, by using tube 7, (or any large tube) and a zigzag motion. Repeat in center of diamond for mounded effect. Press flowers into icing around edge of mound.

COMPLETE CASCADE by pressing in more flowers until mound is covered. Add a few tube 66 leaves.

Many outstanding cakes are trimmed almost entirely with borders and Golden Dream, the cake shown at left, is a splendid example.

Lavish-sized wedding cake tiers give the decorator a perfect opportunity to create interesting sculptural borders. First plan the borders for the base tier, then vary them for the tiers above.

Decorate Golden Dream

Variations of a simply piped border make this cake very impressive. Border elements are repeated on all three tiers for a unified effect.

PREPARE THE TWO-LAYER TIERS. Bake, fill and ice a 16"x4" square tier, a 12"x4" round tier and an 8"x3" round tier. Assemble lower tiers with 14" separator plates and 7½" Corinthian pillars. Use 10" plates and 5" pillars between middle and top tiers. Page 8 shows the method of construction.

PREPARE TRIMS. Pipe tubes 35 and 225 royal icing drop flowers and center each with tube 2. Mount about 30 on wire stems. (See page 14.) Ice a half-ball of styrofoam, attach to upper separator plate and insert stemmed flowers. Glue small plastic doves to 4" Filigree Heart. Glue heart to center of lower separator plate, pipe a heavy curve of icing, press in flowers. Trim ornament with flowers.

PIPE BASE BORDER FOR LOWEST TIER. Only two tubes are used. Pipe a series of puffy garlands using tube 18 and a zigzag motion. Use light pressure as you begin each garland, increase it to center, then decrease pressure at the end. Frame each garland with

tube 14 zigzags. The upper frame rests on the side of the tier, the lower frame on cake board. Pipe a fleur-de-lis between each garland with tube 14. Finish with a rosette at base of fleurs-de-lis with same tube.

The border at top of tier is a variation of the base border. Pipe tube 18 garlands on top of tier, and second garlands on top side. Line up garlands with those at base of tier. Frame the garlands with tube 14 zigzags and drop triple strings with tube 2. Finish with tube 14 rosettes. Frame the separator plate with tube 14 curves.

BASE BORDER OF MIDDLE TIER is done just as the one at base of lowest tier, omitting fleurs-de-lis. Instead, pipe tube 14 fleurs-de-lis on side of tier above every other garland, finishing with rosettes. On top of tier, pipe a tube 18 garland, lining up with garlands at base. Drop tube 2 triple strings and pipe a tube 14 rosette between each garland. Edge separator plate with tube 14.

THE BASE OF TOP TIER is bordered with framed garlands, just as tiers below. Tube 14 fleurs-de-lis are piped on top of cake at edge. Drop a triple tube 2 string drape from point of one fleur-de-lis to the third, omitting one in center. Go back to center fleur-de-lis to start second triple string drape. Continue around tier. Add tube 14 rosettes.

Glue small plastic doves to base of pillars and set ornament on top. Golden Dream serves 196, reserving the 30-serving top tier to freeze for the couple's first anniversary.

13

Flower trims are always lovely on a bridal cake. They can duplicate the blossoms in the bride's bouquet, match the colors of the bridesmaids' dresses or express the season of the year.

FRESH FLOWERS are always a delightful trim—save time for the decorator. Arrange in vases or bowls filled with moistened oasis (keep in refrigerator until ready to place on cake) or in Flower Spikes filled with water from an eye dropper.

PIPED FLOWERS are the special joy of the decorator. Almost any flower can be piped and appear almost real! We recommend piping almost all flowers in royal icing. This icing has many advantages—it insures sharp accurate details, the flowers are easy to handle and may be piped even months in advance. It also allows great flexibility in their arrangement. Only royal icing flowers can be placed securely on cake sides or mounted on wire stems.

Add spikes for cake-side flowers

After piping the flowers on squares of wax paper, set them aside to dry thoroughly. Peel off the wax paper and pipe a royal icing spike on the back with

tube 4 for small and medium-size flowers, tube 6 for large heavy flowers. Let the spike dry. To position, pipe a little icing around the spike, then push the spike into the cake. It will hold the flower firmly to the side.

How to mount flowers on stems

Attaching piped flowers to wire stems adds a whole new dimension to your decorating. You can make bouquets, flower baskets, standing clusters and even natural-looking branches of flowers.

Using green icing and tube 6, pipe a small mound on a square of wax paper. Insert a 6″ length of florists' wire into the mound. Smooth the icing onto the wire with a damp artist's brush. Set into a styrofoam block to dry upright. Add dried piped blossom with a dot of royal icing and set wire into styrofoam to dry again. To attach stems to large heavy flowers, turn flower upside down, pipe icing on its back and set stem on flower. Dry.

PIPING LEAVES ON STEMS. Using royal icing and tube 66, pipe a small anchoring base on wax paper. Lay a 6″ length of florists' wire on this base. Pipe

the leaf over the wire and base so the wire becomes a visible center vein. Allow to dry on the wax paper, then remove. For a rose leaf formation, bind three leaves together with floral tape.

TO MAKE FERNS, bend an 8″ length of florists' wire into a gentle curve. Push the wire into a decorating bag filled with green royal icing and fitted with tube 3. Pull wire out slowly, squeezing bag with steady pressure to cover wire with icing. Lay wire on wax paper and pipe tube 66 leaves, alternating from side to side and jiggling hand for a ruffled effect. Dry, then remove from wax paper.

Decorate Sweetheart Rose

This dainty cake shows how spiked and stemmed flowers can create a spectacular effect.

PIPE THE FLOWERS. Pipe about 90 five-petalled wild roses in two sizes using tubes 103 and 104. Stripe a decorating bag with a little white icing and then fill with pink. Dry, then mount all but ten on wire stems. Pipe royal icing spikes on the remaining wild roses. Pipe about 115 leaves on wires and dry. Tape leaves into clusters of three. Bind the flowers and leaves into one long branch, three short branches and one small cluster with floral tape.

PREPARE THE TIERS. Bake 14″ x 4″ round and 9″ x 3″ heart tiers, each two layers. Fill and ice. Place round tier on an 18″ foil-covered board and stack heart tier on top. (See page 8 for construction.)

DECORATE THE CAKE. Beginning with the base tier, pipe a tube 8 bottom bulb border. Divide side of tier into twelfths. Pipe a tube 104 ruffle garland from point to point. Pipe tube 3 beading along top edge of ruffle. Add tube 7 top bulb border.

On heart tier, pipe tube 5 bottom bulb border. Pipe a tube 104 ruffle over it and add tube 3

beading to ruffle. Pipe tube 4 top bulb border. Mark a 5″ heart on top of tier using smallest Heart Mini-Tier pan or your own pattern. Outline design with tube 4 beading. Pipe tube 2 dots within heart. Divide top of tier into twelfths. Pipe tube 103 ruffle garland from point to point, then add tube 3 beading along inner edge of garland. Secure Petite Bridal Couple on tier top.

ADD FLOWERS. Insert a Flower Spike into the top of each tier. On base tier, insert the wired stems of the long branch and one short branch. On top tier insert stems of remaining two short branches. Secure small cluster at base of top tier. Push spiked flowers into side of cake and trim with tube 66 leaves. Top tier serves 28, base tier serves 92.

How to stage your lovely cake

Give your masterpiece a setting that will really show it off. Usually, the bridal cake is set on a table by itself. Drape the table with a white or pastel cloth, then with a sheer or lace table cloth, both hanging almost to the floor. After the bride and groom have eaten the traditional first slice, the cake is taken away to be cut and served to the guests. For a large cake that requires a rather big table, cover the top of the table with cloth and over-cloth as before, then add a shirred satin table skirt for a dressy touch. (This is easily made.)

If your reception menu consists of cake, nuts and mints with beverages, center the bridal cake on a long table, covered and skirted. On one end arrange the punch bowl and cups, on the other the coffee service. Allow plenty of space for plates, forks, napkins and compotes of nuts and mints.

If you are serving a groom's cake, place it with the bridal cake or on a separate sweet table. In the past, this cake was cut and put in small boxes for guests to take home, but in recent years, the groom's cake is served to the guests.

Flower arrangements, of course, add a lovely touch. If the cake itself is trimmed with flowers, tall palms or ferns set behind the table will provide a graceful setting. For after-four receptions, candles add to the festive occasion.

CHAPTER TWO

A collection of elegant cakes especially designed for large formal receptions

The cakes in this chapter are the joy of the dedicated decorator. Inventive in construction and technique, each is a true masterpiece. All are planned to serve a large number of guests.

Summer Splendor

Absolutely spectacular! Crowned by a sparkling fountain and graced by dozens of ruffled petunias, Summer Splendor is impressive in size and beguiling in its fluffy feminine appearance.

MAKE FLOWERS IN ADVANCE. Line a 1⅝″ lily nail with foil. Using tube 102 with narrow end up and royal icing, start piping the petal deep inside nail. Move up to outer edge then back down to starting point, jiggling hand for ruffled effect. Make five petals. Pipe tube 14 green star in center and push in a few artificial stamens. When dry, peel off foil. You'll need about 200. Pipe spikes on back of most flowers (page 14). Paint four Twin Angels ornaments with thinned royal icing and dry.

PREPARE TIERS. For fountain tier, cut a 10″ circle from center of a 12″ x 4″ round styrofoam dummy. Line with foil, then ice outer sides and top edge. Place on 14″ round separator plate and position Kolor-Flo Fountain inside. Bake, ice and assemble the tiers as shown in the diagram using twelve ½″ dowel rods in base tier for support. (See page 8.)

DECORATE CAKE, beginning with bottom tier. Divide each side into thirds. Mark Beautiful Bridal scallop pattern with a toothpick on sides. At each division and at the corners, pipe columns with tube 8B. Add two swirls to the top of each column with tube 4B, two smaller swirls and a rosette with tube 32. Using tube 22, pipe zigzag base border. Pipe scallop pattern, rosettes and fleurs-de-lis with tube 17. Reverse shell top border is piped with tube 32.

On 18″ square tier, pipe bottom border of tube 19 rosettes. On each side of tier, make a mark every 1½″, leaving space in center open. Pipe tube 16 strings from point to point. Top intersections with tube 17 rosettes. Pipe top shell border with tube 19. Attach a Twin Angels ornament on each side.

Divide 16″ round tier into eighths. At each point, pipe a tube 199 upright shell. Top each with a tube 17 fleur-de-lis. Pipe tube 19 shells between each upright shell for bottom border. Mark scallop pattern on side of tier with a toothpick. Pipe scallops and add rosettes with tube 17. Top shell border is piped with tube 19 and lower separator plate is edged with the same tube. Secure Kissing Lovebirds ornament to separator plate with royal icing. Set 7½″ Corinthian pillars on plate.

Divide side of fountain tier into twelfths. At each division pipe an upright shell with tube 32, then fill in between them at base of tier with tube 19 shells. Drop double tube 14 strings between the tops of the upright shells and add tube 16 rosettes. Pipe top border of tube 18 reverse shells. Around inner edge, pipe tube 4B shells with a tube 17 rosette between each. Glue Cupid with Arrow to fountain.

ADD FINISHING TOUCHES. Attach the flowers on all tiers on mounds of icing as pictured. Add tube 67 leaves. Wire the electrical fountain cord down the back of a pillar. Summer Splendor serves 846.

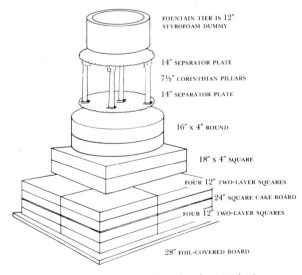

FOUNTAIN TIER IS 12″ STYROFOAM DUMMY

14″ SEPARATOR PLATE

7½″ CORINTHIAN PILLARS

14″ SEPARATOR PLATE

16″ x 4″ ROUND

18″ x 4″ SQUARE

FOUR 12″ TWO-LAYER SQUARES

24″ SQUARE CAKE BOARD

FOUR 12″ TWO-LAYER SQUARES

28″ FOIL-COVERED BOARD

(When serving, cut base tier as two tiers.)

This magnificent showpiece will be the star of the most formal and lavish wedding reception—and an artistic achievement for the serious decorator.

Cathedral is crowned by a soaring gum paste ornament that rests on a windowed drum. Only the three lower tiers are constructed of cake. For the drum and ornament, use styrofoam for support, rolled gum paste for cover and royal icing for glue and trim. *All styrofoam pieces must be painted with thinned royal icing* and dried before gum paste is applied. Recipe for gum paste is on page 128. Transfer patterns to light cardboard.

First make gum paste trims

MAKE FLOWERS—30 roses, 150 briar roses and 75 violets using Flower Garden Cutters and following the instruction booklet. Make all without stems.

CUT PIECES FOR DRUM AND ORNAMENT following directions on patterns. Dry all about 24 hours. Cut styrofoam pieces, paint with icing and dry.

Assemble gum paste pieces

SECURE DRUM INNER WINDOWS to outer windows, then fill crevices with icing. Pipe tube 1 designs.

SECURE THE THREE SHELF LAYERS together. Assemble the shelf supports on the shelf base layer. Fill crevices with icing and dry. Pipe tube 1 trims. Attach inner green panels to shelf backdrops. Dry, then pipe tube 1s cornelli lace on panels. Complete trim on backdrops with tube 1. Secure a Winged Angel to each. Dry thoroughly.

Continued on page 21

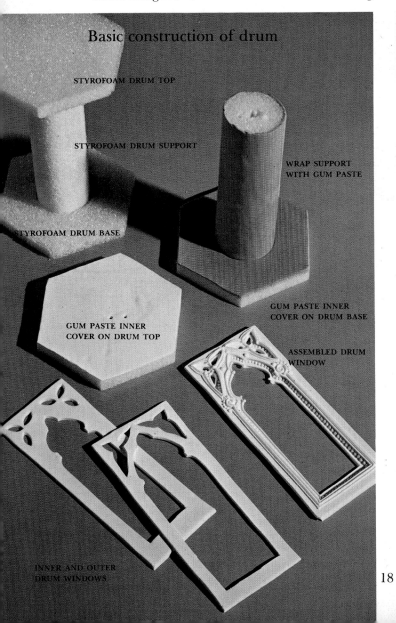

Basic construction of drum

STYROFOAM DRUM TOP

STYROFOAM DRUM SUPPORT

STYROFOAM DRUM BASE

WRAP SUPPORT WITH GUM PASTE

GUM PASTE INNER COVER ON DRUM TOP

GUM PASTE INNER COVER ON DRUM BASE

ASSEMBLED DRUM WINDOW

INNER AND OUTER DRUM WINDOWS

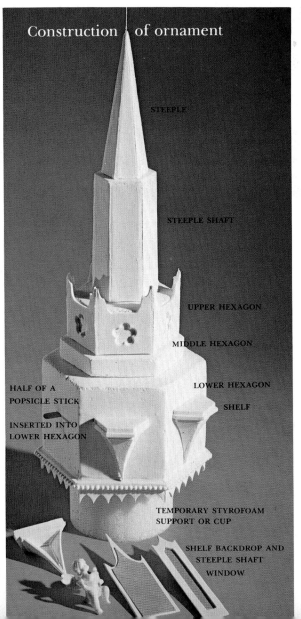

Construction of ornament

STEEPLE

STEEPLE SHAFT

UPPER HEXAGON

MIDDLE HEXAGON

LOWER HEXAGON

SHELF

HALF OF A POPSICLE STICK

INSERTED INTO LOWER HEXAGON

TEMPORARY STYROFOAM SUPPORT OR CUP

SHELF BACKDROP AND STEEPLE SHAFT WINDOW

18

19

STEEPLE
ON STEEPLE SHAFT

UPPER HEXAGON

LOWER HEXAGON

WINDOWED DRUM

ATTACH GREEN PANELS behind openings in steeple shaft windows. Pipe tube 1s cornelli lace on panels.

Assemble drum and ornament

PUT DRUM TOGETHER. Roll green gum paste very thin and cut a 6″ high x 6¾″ long rectangle. Brush iced support with egg white and wrap paste around, trimming excess. Stand support on end and place green gum paste inner cover on top, then styrofoam drum base. Carefully drive a long nail through into the support. Turn support over and attach white gum paste inner cover and styrofoam drum top the same way. Attach windows around drum to styrofoam top and base. On wax paper pipe two tube 4 lines, 7″ long, next to each other, then add a third line on top. Pipe six sets, dry, then attach along window seams. Dry.

PREPARE LOWER HEXAGON. Ice lower hexagon smoothly and dry. Attach lower hexagon bottom plate and fill crevices. Turn so plate is on top. Pipe a line of icing on bottom of cornices and attach around edge of plate. Fill seams with icing, smooth and dry. Turn lower hexagon over and place on a cup or temporary styrofoam support so cornices are not damaged. Pipe tube 1 trim on cornices. Insert a half popsicle stick into each side of lower hexagon, 1¾″ below top edge so ¾″ protrudes to support shelves. On wax paper, pipe two tube 4 lines, 4″ long, next to each other, then add a third line on top. Pipe six sets and dry. Attach to corners of lower hexagon. Pipe tube 3 triple bead border around top edge, tube 2 beading around base and edge of gum paste plate. Ice middle hexagon and dry, then secure on top of lower hexagon.

ICE UPPER HEXAGON smoothly and dry. Secure upper hexagon disc in center of top and edge with tube 2 beading. Secure the side walls around upper hexagon and fill all crevices with icing. Dry, then pipe tube 1 beading around top edge of walls. Add designs with tube 1 and pipe a tube 3 line between the walls. Around windows, pipe tube 1 designs. Pipe tube 2 dots at top points of walls.

ADD CORNER POINTS AND SHELVES. Secure lower hexagon to top of drum. Mount six pairs of large corner points on the gum paste plate directly above cornices with lines of icing. Dry, then trim with tube 1. Secure upper hexagon to middle hexagon. Attach the pairs of small corner points to top edge of middle hexagon. Dry, add tube 1 trim. Secure remaining pairs of large corner points to top edge of lower hexagon, dry, and pipe trim with tube 1. Attach shelves to sticks on lower hexagon.

PREPARE STEEPLE. Secure an 8″ piece of florists' wire to inner side of one steeple point so about 2″ protrudes from top. Assemble steeple points around steeple base. Fill crevices with icing and dry. Next, assemble steeple shaft. Attach three steeple sides to one steeple shaft plate with royal icing. Lay shaft on its side and attach the other steeple shaft plate, then the three other sides. Stand upright, fill crevices, smooth and dry.

Secure steeple to steeple shaft and dry. Then lay on its side and pipe ornamentation on seams with tube 1. Stand upright. Insert wire at peak into a decorating bag fitted with tube 2 to coat with icing. Add trims with tube 1 and dry. Attach shaft windows, then secure steeple to upper hexagon disc.

FINAL ASSEMBLY. Secure shelf backdrops to lower hexagon. Attach a Musical Trio cherub to each gum paste pedestal and pipe tube 2 beading around seam. Secure within windows of drum.

Decorate the cake

BAKE TIERS, ice and assemble on a serving plate as shown in diagram below. Use ½″ dowels in tiers when assembling (see page 8). Center a 6″ hexagon separator plate on top of 12″ tier with studs for attaching pillars down and mark. Insert dowel rods into top tier to support ornament. Push plate down until flat against cake surface. Paint six Angelinos with thinned royal icing and dry. Divide side of bottom tier into twelfths. At each division, trace trefoil design with a toothpick. Pipe design using tubes 5 and 6. Pipe triple ball borders, using tube 10 for bottom and tube 8 for top.

ON SECOND TIER, trace window pattern on sides. Pipe triple ball border around base of tier with tube 6 and single ball border around top. Pipe designs around windows with tubes 2 and 3. Pipe two tube 4 lines next to each other down the sides of the design, then pipe third line on top.

ON TOP TIER, mark gothic design and pipe with tubes 4 and 5. Pipe tube 4 triple ball border around base of tier and single ball border around top. Secure an Angelino to each side with icing.

ATTACH FLOWERS in garland shapes on the middle tier. Pipe tube 3 ribbons at the intersections of the garlands. On the top tier, attach flowers in a cluster on each top corner within the piped design. Secure ornament to separator plate on top of cake with royal icing. Cathedral serves 282 guests.

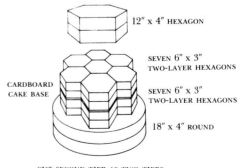

12″ x 4″ HEXAGON

SEVEN 6″ x 3″
TWO-LAYER HEXAGONS

CARDBOARD
CAKE BASE

SEVEN 6″ x 3″
TWO-LAYER HEXAGONS

18″ x 4″ ROUND

CUT SECOND TIER AS TWO TIERS

PINK CRYSTAL, SHINING SHOWPIECE

Pink candy hearts glitter like jewels on this sparkling cake, grand in size, but dainty in effect. A lighted fountain, set in a decorated base, is placed on either side to create an enchanting setting.

MAKE TRIMS. Pipe tube 102 and 103 daisies. Add tube 4 centers and flatten with a fingertip dipped in edible glitter. Dry within curved surface.

Make about 160 pink hard candy hearts (see page 128). Attach around Petite Diamond Crown ornament with royal icing. Pipe dots of pink piping gel on the rings above the bridal couple. Attach small ribbon bows and candy hearts to the hands of Dancing Angel and two Cherub Card-Holders. Glue cherubs to petite heart plate.

Prepare styrofoam dummy cakes for fountains as described on page 17. Set on cake boards. Glue Cherub Card-Holders to the tops of the fountains.

PREPARE TIERS. Bake 18″, 16″, 14″, 10″ and 6″ round, two-layer tiers each 4″ high. Fill, ice and assemble on a 22″ board. Elevate top tiers with 10″ separator plates and 7½″ Corinthian pillars.

DECORATE TIERS. On 18″ tier, pipe tube 22 bottom shell border and tube 17 top shell border. Ring base with candy hearts. Divide tier into sixths and mark a curve for flower garland in each division. Pipe bows at ends of curves with tube 1 and pink piping gel. Secure daisies in garland shape.

On 16″ tier, pipe tube 19 reverse shell bottom border and tube 17 top shell border. Mark six curves around sides and secure candy hearts and daisies.

On 14″ tier, pipe tube 16 bottom shell border and add "C"-shaped scrolls over it. Pipe tube 17 top shell border. Pipe six pink piping gel bows with tube 1 on side of tiers. Secure a candy heart to each of the streamers. Arrange daisies between bows. Edge separator plate with tube 16. Secure ornament and trim pillar bases with daisies.

On 10″ tier, pipe tube 18 shells around base and tube 17 reverse shells around top. Secure daisies and hearts to front and back of tier.

On 6″ tier, pipe tube 17 bottom shell border and tube 16 reverse shell top border. Place Dancing Angel on top of tier and surround with daisies. Attach clusters of flowers.

DECORATE FOUNTAIN DUMMIES. With royal icing, pipe tube 19 bottom shell borders and tube 17 reverse shell top borders. Attach six plastic Lacy Hearts and secure a candy heart in the center of each. Add daisies between hearts. Without the 16-serving top tier, Pink Crystal serves 406 guests.

23

Prelude is the very image of what a wedding cake ought to be—rose trimmed, ruffled and crowned with a flowery heart. Four surrounding heart cakes provide ample servings for a very large reception. For more servings, decorate additional heart cakes and bring out as needed.

Make trims in advance

ROMANTIC WHITE ROSES are the featured trim on Prelude, and they are used lavishly! Pipe them ahead in royal icing and dry—then the rest of the decorating goes quickly. Here are the quantities you'll need—note that many roses require icing spikes piped on the back. (See page 14.)

> FOR BASE TIER: Twelve tube 104 roses.
> FOR MIDDLE TIER: Eight tube 103 roses plus 40 buds, all with spikes.
> FOR TOP TIER: Six tube 102 roses plus twelve buds, all with spikes.
> FOR HEART ORNAMENT: Twelve tube 103 roses plus six buds.
> FOR HEART CAKES: 112 tube 103 roses and about two dozen buds. Pipe spikes on 64 of the roses.

PREPARE THE TOP ORNAMENT. Make gum paste as directed on page 128. Let it age overnight, then roll out to a thickness of about ⅛". Cut a gum paste heart with a 4" heart cutter, then remove the center with a 2½" heart cutter to create an open frame. Dry flat at least 24 hours. Twist two pieces of heavy florists' wire into a "Y" shape, each arm about 2½" long, stem about 3½" long. Attach the wire to the back of the frame with royal icing so the stem extends down from the heart at the point. Dry. Cut a second gum paste heart frame exactly the same as the first, but do not dry. Brush the back of the dried heart with egg white and press the wet heart to it, matching the edges. Dry thoroughly, then wrap the exposed wire with floral tape. Attach tube 103 roses and buds to the heart frame with dots of royal icing. Add tube 66 leaves and set aside to dry.

Prepare the tiers

Bake all the tiers needed for the entire cake. Bake four 9" x 4" hearts, a 14" x 4", a 10" x 4" and a 6" x 3" round—each two layers high. Fill and ice.

Prelude is constructed on the Lace Cake Stand. See page 9 for directions. Place heart cakes on cardboard cake bases the same size and shape. Place round tiers on matching cake circles with center hole cut out. Fill and ice all tiers.

Set each heart cake on a 10" plate, then set plate on an 8" cake pan to steady for decorating. Cut center holes in the 14" and 10" tiers with Cake Corer Tube. Set the 14" and 10" round tiers on corresponding 16" and 12" plates, then on cake pans the size of the baked tier to steady the plates.

Decorate the tiers

ON 14" TIER, pipe tube 4B bottom shell border and add tube 104 fluted ribbon. Divide side of tier into twelfths. Drop a string guideline from point to point. Following guideline, pipe a tube 104 ruffle, then a tube 16 zigzag and top with tube 2 strings. Add a third string above garland. Pipe tube 16 top shell border. Attach tube 104 roses on top of tier and add tube 67 leaves.

DIVIDE 10" TIER into eighths. Pipe tube 18 bottom shell border. Drop a string guideline on side of cake from one marked division to the next, then pipe a tube 104 ruffle following the guide. Add a tube 16 zigzag and top with tube 2 strings. Then drop another string above the garland. Pipe tube 16 top shell border. Push spiked tube 103 roses and buds into the side of tier at the intersections of the garlands. Add tube 66 leaves.

DECORATE THE HEART CAKES. Pipe tube 18 reverse shell border around the base and add a tube 16 top shell border. Sketch a heart shape with a toothpick on top of cake and extending down sides. Form garland by setting tube 103 roses on top of cake on mounds of icing and pushing spiked roses into sides. Trim with tube 66 leaves.

Assemble the cake

Add 6½" column to 4-Arm Support; then 14" decorated tier and 7¾" column. Pipe tube 16 border around column. Now put 10" decorated tier and 7¾" column in position and edge column with tube 16. Secure 8" plate with nut and add top 6" tier.

DECORATE 6" TIER. Pipe a tube 16 bottom shell border. Divide side into sixths. Drop a string from one marked division to the next, then pipe a tube 104 ruffle following this guideline. Pipe a tube 16 zigzag and top with tube 2 strings. Add tube 16 top shell border. Push in spiked tube 102 roses and rosebuds. Add tube 65 leaves. Insert wire on top ornament into cake so it stands upright.

Without the 16-serving top tier, Prelude serves 252 guests.

Pink as a rosy sunrise, pretty as the bridesmaids and feminine as the fluffy carnation trim—that's Morning Song. This stunning cake is planned for a very large reception, but if you need even more servings than it provides, decorate additional satellite cakes to bring out as required. Many brides like to present identical cakes to the parents.

Make flowers in advance

Pipe tube 10 balls of icing on small squares of wax paper and let icing set. These will be the bases on which the carnation petals are piped so they will have a full, fluffy look. Secure the wax paper square to a number 7 flower nail with a dot of icing. Stripe decorating bag with a small amount of white icing, then fill with deep pink. Using tube 104, begin to pipe petals around the base of the ball, jiggling hand for a ruffled effect. Move up the ball piping more rows of petals, each progressively shorter and more upturned until the petals at the top are almost straight up. You will need about five dozen carnations. When dry, secure several carnations to Hearts Take Wing ornament with icing. This will be placed within the arched pillars.

Decorate the tiers

Bake two-layer round tiers—8" x 3", 12" x 4", 16" x 4". In addition, bake six two-layer 10" cakes. Fill the layers, then ice the tiers smoothly. Place 16" tier on the 18" separator plate from the Arched Pillar Tier Set. Secure the pillars to the second separator plate and place the 16" tier on top of them. Raise 12" tier with 14" separator plates and 5" Grecian pillars. Use 10" separator plates and 5" Grecian pillars below the top 8" tier. Place each of the 10" cakes on a 14" foil-covered cake board.

DECORATE 16" TIER. Divide the side of the tier into sixteenths and pipe a tube 32 upright shell at each division. Pipe tube 19 shells between them to complete the bottom border. Drop a triple tube 3 string drape between the upright shells and add a tube 19 star at the top of the upright shells. Pipe a tube 16 fleur-de-lis above every other set of strings. Edge the lower separator plate that rests on top of tier with tube 16 and pipe top shell border on tier with tube 17.

DECORATE 12" TIER. Divide side of tier into eighths and pipe a tube 32 upright shell at each division. Fill space between them with tube 17 shells. Between upright shells, mark heart shapes with a 2" heart cutter. Pipe design with tube 17, adding curved flourishes. Drop triple tube 3 strings from tops of upright shells and finish with tube 17 stars. Edge separator plate on top of tier with tube 15. Circle top of tier with tube 16 shells.

DECORATE 8" TIER. Pipe tube 17 bottom shell border. Divide side of tier into eighths. Pipe a tube 17 fleur-de-lis at each point, then drop tube 3 double strings from the base of each one. Add tube 17 stars. Pipe tube 16 top shell border.

ADD THE FINISHING TOUCHES. Secure ornament between the Arched Pillars with icing. Glue a ribbon bow to each pillar and then glue three 1" filigree bells below the ribbon. Pipe a mound of icing on separator plate on 16" tier, and arrange carnations. Trim with tube 68 leaves. Add a ribbon bow. Make an identical flower arrangement on top of 12" tier. On 16" tier, secure a White Bird between each pair of pillars with icing. Glue a Bridal Couple to a plastic heart base and place on top of cake. Surround the ornament base with carnations and trim with tube 68 leaves.

Decorate the satellite cakes

Each of the six 10" round cakes is decorated the same way. Cut a 10" circle of paper, fold it into tenths and cut a scallop pattern. Trace the pattern onto the top of the cake with a toothpick, connecting the inner points of the scallops to the ones across with lines. Pipe the design with tube 13. Add tube 17 stars at the intersections of the piped lines. Pipe ten tube 32 upright shells at base of cake. Pipe tube 17 shells between them to complete the bottom border. Drop a series of three tube 3 strings from the tops of the upright shells. Add tube 17 stars. Pipe the top shell border with tube 16.

Pipe a mound of icing on top of cake and press in carnations to create a fluffy flower arrangement. Add tube 68 leaves and a ribbon bow. Decorate each of the other cakes the same way. Place the six cakes around the base of the main cake. Top tier of main cake serves 30. Lower tiers and six satellite cakes serve 474 guests.

MARLA wore a glittering $2 million diamond tiara.

PHOTO EXCLUSIVE

friend
of his baby
fany.

"This is the biggest, clas
est wedding New York has
seen in decades!" Trump
told me while enjoying his
December 20 nuptials.

The star-studded ceremo-
ny took place in the Gran
Ballroom of Trump's Plaz
hotel in New York — ironica
ly, the hotel that Trump's
wife Ivana redecorated
ran before their break

The ballroom seate
dreds, but hundreds
the 1,000-plus g
packed standing
available foot

Celebritys
soap star
shock jo
anca
O'D
M

sports
cluding
champio
field, forme
zier, O.J. Sim
moter Don Kin

But conspicuo
absence were Trum
children by Ivana. T
pected them to con
learned before the we
that Donny, 16, Ivanka,
and 9-year-old Eric would
main in Aspen, Colo., whe
they were vacationing w
Ivana.

The Grand Ballroom
decorated with thousan
white orchids. On the s
the ceremony was to
was an arch formed b
lings intertwined with
dripping with crystal

The wedding was
8:00 p.m., but it was
8:40 that the bride
families were seate

**LET 'EM EAT CAKE: Marla feeds her
hubby a piece of their 6-foot-high wedding cake. Then the happy couple
washed it down with champagne (left).**

Golden Spring is a sunny towering centerpiece for a very large reception. Guests will marvel at the beautiful gum paste lilies that look as if they had been freshly picked! Present the lasting flower clusters to the bridesmaids and to the mothers of the bride and groom.

Make the golden lilies

Create the beautiful gum paste lilies with their leaves using Flower Garden Cutters and the instructions that come with the set. (You'll be surprised at how quickly and easily these "one piece" flowers go together.) You'll need about 40 lilies and 8 buds. When dry, bind the leaves to the lilies with floral tape. Make five clusters by taping five lilies and a bud together. Tie a bow to each. Reserve four lilies to trim the ornament and set aside the rest for a bouquet below the top tier.

Prepare the fountain

Paint ten Filigree Shields with thinned royal icing and dry. Make fountain collar from a 12" styrofoam circle, 2" high. Cut a 10" circle from the center. Paint the collar, in and out with thinned royal icing. Dry thoroughly. Secure the filigree shields around the outside of the collar with small mounds of royal icing, alternating the shields so the point of one is up and the point of the next is down. Dry, then pipe tube 18 stars around base.

Decorate the cake

BAKE THE TIERS. Bake four 12" x 4" square, one 16" x 4" round, one 12" x 4" hexagon and one 8" x 3" round tier, each two layers high. Fill all layers. Ice two adjacent sides of each 12" square tier. Assemble the four tiers on a 28" cake board, iced sides touching to form a 24" square tier. Ice remaining tiers. Assemble the 16" round and 12" hexagon tiers on the Arched Pillar Tier Set, and raise the top tier with 9" hexagon separator plates and six 5" Grecian pillars. Take tiers apart to decorate.

DECORATE BASE TIER. Using 2½" cutters, mark a heart at each corner and one in the center on each side of tier. Pipe bottom shell border with tube 4B. Pipe hearts with tube 16, adding curved shell flourishes. Pipe tube 22 top shell border.

DECORATE SECOND TIER. Divide side of 16" tier into sixths and mark an upside down heart at each division using 2½" cutters. Pipe tube 22 bottom shell border. Pipe heart designs with tube 16, adding curved flourishes. Pipe tube 18 top shell border.

TRIM HEXAGON TIER. Use 2½" cutter again to mark hexagon. Pipe tube 18 bottom shell border. Outline heart shapes with tube 16, adding curved shell flourishes. Edge separator plate on top of the tier with tube 16. Pipe tube 17 shells down sides of tier and around the top.

DECORATE TOP TIER. Divide the side of the tier into sixths. At each division, mark a heart so one is right side up and next is upside down using a 2" cutter. Pipe bottom shell border with tube 17, then outline the hearts with tube 16 and add curving shells . Pipe top shell border with tube 16.

ADD FINISHING TOUCHES. Make several holes in the lower 9" hexagon separator plate with a heated ice pick or nail. Insert the stems of individual lilies through the holes. Reassemble the cake, positioning the fountain within the Arched Pillars before placing the 16" tier in position.

Remove the flowers from inside the bell of the Wedding Chime ornament. Insert two lilies into the bell, securing them with mounds of icing. Then secure a lily on each side of the bell. Secure the ornament to the top of the cake.

On the base tier, insert a Flower Spike into each corner of the tier top. Place a cluster of lilies in each Flower Spike and one in front of cake. Top tier serves 30, remaining tiers serve 456.

30

Exquisite gum paste figures of the wedding party are a beautiful memento for the happy couple. Duplicate the dress of the members of the wedding party for an especially personal touch.

Create gum paste trims

Make many briar roses and leaves with the Flower Garden Cutter Set following instructions that come with the set. Mount about half of them on wire stems. Tape stemmed flowers into one large and one small spray for top ornament and six small clusters to form wreath around top tier. In addition, make three dozen forget-me-nots. Mold four Baroque mold Angelica designs, dry and pipe a royal icing spike on the back of each. Make a 2¾" and a 3" diameter circle from ¼" wide gum paste strips. Dry and secure to Petite Heart Base. Cut swags for upper separator plate using Beautiful Bridal pattern and the method on page 97.

Mold gum paste figures

Create the lovely, detailed figures using Wilton People Molds and the instruction booklet that accompanies them. Mold the figures and follow the directions for making and attaching clothing. See

Continued on next page

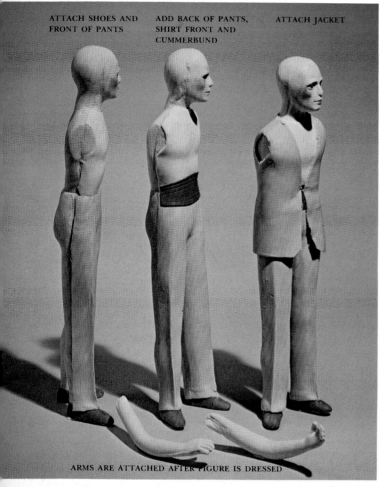

ATTACH SHOES AND
FRONT OF PANTS

ADD BACK OF PANTS,
SHIRT FRONT AND
CUMMERBUND

ATTACH JACKET

ARMS ARE ATTACHED AFTER FIGURE IS DRESSED

ATTACH SHOES
AND BODICE

ADD UNDERSKIRT

ATTACH SKIRT

ARMS ARE ATTACHED
AFTER FIGURE IS DRESSED

special instructions below. Patterns needed are in the Beautiful Bridal collection.

GROOM. Shirt front is a 1¾″ x 1⅞″ piece of gum paste. Jacket sleeves are 4″ x 1¾″ pieces. Add extra pieces at the shoulders after the arms are attached and dried for a padded, squared-off appearance. Smooth with fingers to blend with jacket.

BRIDE. Attach and dry underskirt, then add skirt. Add overskirt of tulle and secure at top back with a small stitch. Pull down to fit smoothly. Pipe embroidery with tube 1. Spray overskirt and veil with clear acrylic spray. Hand-model prayer book.

FLOWER GIRL. Dress figure, making a high-waisted bodice. Hand-model basket and dry. Add florists' wire handle with royal icing and secure forget-me-nots in basket. Attach to hand.

RING BEARER. Trim feet to create heels before drying leg section. Dress figure. Hand-model pillow and add royal icing rings. Secure to hands.

Bake and decorate tiers

Prepare two 13″ square separator plates. Glue stud plate at each corner on flat sides. Cut a 12″ square from 1/16″ thick pink gum paste. Attach to lower plate with egg white, cutting holes for stud plates. On upper plate, at every fifth scallop on edge, make holes for wires of swags with a heated nail. Bake, fill and ice 18″ x 4″ square, 12″ x 4″ square and 8″ x 3″ round, two-layer tiers. Place bottom tier on a sturdy 22″ foil-covered board. Pipe shell borders on all tiers using tubes 18 and 17 on bottom tier, tube 17 on middle tier and tube 16 on top tier. Pipe garland on bottom tier using tubes 127, 18 and 4, on middle tier using tubes 104, 17 and 3.

Assemble Wedding Party

Assemble tiers using the prepared separator plates and 10¼″ Roman pillars. Determine positions of the bride and groom on the gum paste carpet and mark. Make holes with a heated nail for the wires extending from bottoms of feet. Position bride and groom, inserting the wires into the holes. Secure ring ornament to top of cake. Insert wires on swags into holes in upper separator plate. Secure unstemmed flowers and bows to swags with royal icing. Trim tier sides with flowers.

Insert six Flower Spikes around base of top tier, and fill with flower clusters in wreath effect. Set double ring ornament on cake, insert spike behind it, and fill with flower sprays. Insert the wires on the feet of the ring bearer and flower girl through small pieces of iced cardboard. Set figures on cake. Conceal cardboard with more icing. Figures can be removed from the cake and the wires on the feet pushed into a square of 1″ styrofoam, iced with royal icing. This will be the bride's keepsake. Without the 30-serving top tier, Wedding Party serves 234 guests.

32

CHAPTER THREE

A bouquet of flowering cakes that express young love in every season

Flowers are the favorite trim for wedding cakes. Brides love them because their delicate colors and forms can echo the blossoms in their bouquets. Decorators love them because artistically piped flowers really show off their skill and seem to trim the tiers almost by themselves.

Leaf through this chapter to find your favorite, from January's dainty snowdrop to Christmas holly. All of the cakes are of medium size, serving 110 to over 200 guests.

We begin with the rose, love's own flower, that knows no season except romance.

ANNIVERSARY ROSE. Directions on page 34.

33

Anniversary rose *(shown on page 33)*

Traditional in its rosy trim but very new and unusual in its structure, Anniversary Rose holds a happy surprise within its pillars—a miniature cake to freeze and serve on the first anniversary!

MAKE ROSES AND BUDS in varied pinks, using tubes 102, 103, 104 and 124. Dry, then pipe a tube 5 royal icing spike on the backs of about one-fourth of them to push into the sides of the tiers.

PREPARE TWO-LAYER TIERS. Bake 12" x 18" x 4" rectangle, 10" x 3" square and 5" x 3" round tiers. Fill and ice. Place bottom tier on a foil-covered cake board, 10" tier on an 11" square separator plate and 5" tier on a 6" cake board. The top tier is set to one side of the base rectangular tier. Mark position of pillars on base tier, with an 11" square separator plate. Set a 7½" Corinthian pillar on each mark and push a ¼" dowel rod through each pillar down to cake board. Mark top of pillars on dowels, lift and clip off ⅞" below marks. Push dowels back down to cake board.

DECORATE TIERS. For base border on bottom tier, pipe tube 18 upright shells. Add a star between each shell. Drop a double tube 2 string from the top of every other shell, then from remaining shells. Pipe tube 17 reverse shell top border.

On top tier, pipe tube 17 reverse shell bottom border. Divide each side of tier into tenths at top. Drop double tube 2 strings from every other point, then drop strings from remaining points. Pipe tube 17 rosette top border.

On tiny anniversary cake, pipe tube 17 reverse shell bottom border. Divide top edge of tier into sixths and drop tube 2 strings from point to point. Add a tube 17 top shell border. Pipe names with tube 2. Trim with roses and tube 67 leaves.

ASSEMBLE CAKE. Place anniversary cake between pillars, then add top tier. Attach roses to bottom tier. Secure Moonbeam ornament to top tier and trim with small roses and buds. Add more roses to upper tier to form a cascade. Pipe tube 67 leaves. Cake serves 158 wedding guests.

Rose Romance *(Shown on opposite page)*

Sentimental and frilly, this is the perfect cake for the bride who loves romantic traditions.

MAKE FLOWERS IN ADVANCE. Pipe about four dozen roses and buds using tubes 102 and 103. Dry, then pipe a tube 5 royal icing spike on the backs of about half the roses. Dry thoroughly.

BAKE TWO-LAYER TIERS. Bake 18" x 4", 14" x 4" and 8" x 3" round tiers. Fill, ice and assemble on a 22", foil-covered cake board. Elevate the top tier with Cupid Pillar Separator Set.

DECORATE BASE TIER. Divide tier into sixteenths, marking the side 2" up from the base. At each division, pipe a tube 4B upright shell from the base to the mark. Fill in the base border with tube 4B stars. Drop a tube 5 guideline from shell to shell. Pipe over guideline with a tube 14 zigzag, then add tube 3 strings. Pipe a tube 3 bow at the top of each upright shell. Drop string guidelines from top edge of tier, lining up with base border. Pipe tube 14 "e" motion garlands over guidelines, and add scallops on top of tier. Finish with tube 67 leaves.

ON MIDDLE TIER, pipe tube 4B bottom shell border and drape with tube 3 string. Divide top edge into sixteenths and drop a string guideline from point to point. Pipe a garland over the guideline with tube 4 using a circular motion. Add scallops with the same tube on the top of the tier. Drop four tube 3 strings on the garland and add tube 67 leaves. Edge separator plate with tube 4.

DECORATE TOP TIER with tube 3. Pipe bottom bead border. Divide the side of the tier into twelfths and pipe a garland from point to point so it extends over the bottom border. Drop one string on the garland and two above it. Pipe a bow at the intersections of the strings and a tube 67 leaf at points of the garlands. Pipe the top border the same as the middle tier, but drop only a single string.

ADD THE FINISHING TOUCHES. Attach clusters of three roses at every other scallop on base tier. Secure roses to a mound of icing between the pillars. Attach buds around feet of cupids and add tube 65 leaves. Glue Kissing Lovebirds to Heart Base. Place ornament on cake top and secure roses around the base with icing. Trim all roses with tube 67 leaves. If the bride saves the 30-serving top tier for the first anniversary, remaining tiers will serve 240 wedding guests.

The delicate snowdrop trims this snow-white cake for a January wedding. Impressive-looking but easy-to-pipe borders complete the airy effect.

Make flowers first

Make the snowdrops ahead of time with royal icing, then decorating will go quickly. You need about 70 flowers and buds and 27 leaves.

FOR FLOWERS, bend one end of a 6″ length of florists' wire into a hook. Insert through tube 6 into a decorating bag, squeeze lightly and pull out a ½″ long, slender green bulb. Push into a styrofoam block to dry. Pipe three cupped white petals about halfway up bulb with tube 81. Pipe three tube 80 outer petals. Pipe some flowers in closed position, others open and some with petals curved outward. Bend wire sharply below bulb and pipe a green tube 2 spur just below bend.

To MAKE BUDS, insert dried bulb into decorating bag fitted with tube 8 and pull out to a point. Bend wire below bud and add tube 2 spur.

FOR LEAVES, curve 6″ lengths of florists' wire and insert into decorating bag fitted with tube 65. Pull out wire while squeezing for a slender, tapered leaf. Set in styrofoam block to dry.

MAKE VASE AND BASKETS. Glue a 2″ plastic bell to the top plate of the Petite Heart Base, dry, then paint with thinned royal icing. Line with clear plastic, fill with royal icing, then insert snowdrops and leaves into the bell. For side arrangements, create four baskets by gluing a 4″ Filigree Heart to back of a plastic Curved Triangle. Dry, then paint with thinned royal icing.

Decorate the cake

PREPARE THE TIERS. Bake 14″ x 4″, 10″ x 4″ and 6″ x 3″ square, two-layer tiers. Fill and ice the tiers. Assemble on an 18″ square, foil-covered cake board. Raise top tier with 7″ square separator plates and four 5″ Corinthian pillars. Before placing top tier in position, thread ¼″ ribbon through loop of a 2″ bell. Insert ribbon ends into tops of two pillars, diagonally across plate, and tape in place. Add bow to bell, then set top tier in place.

DECORATE LOWER TIERS. On base tier, pipe tube 17 bottom shell border. Divide each side into sixths, drop string guideline, and pipe a tube 17 zigzag garland from point to point. Trim with tube 3 strings and fleurs-de-lis.

On middle tier, pipe tube 16 shells around the base. Starting 1″ from each corner, divide each side into sixths. Pipe tube 16 zigzag garlands from point to point, leaving the center section empty. Trim garlands with tube 3 strings. Edge separator plate on top of tier with tube 16 and pipe top shell border with the same tube. Pipe a "V" of icing on the back of the heart baskets and push onto cake, holding until icing sets.

Now pipe top border on base tier. Mark six scallops on each side on top of tier and pipe with tube 103, making a ruffle. Pipe a tube 17 zigzag garland, filling each ruffle scallop, then pipe a matching zigzag garland directly below on the side of the tier. Drop a pair of tube 3 strings beneath the garlands and add a bow.

ON TOP TIER, pipe tube 16 zigzag garlands around base and add a tube 5 dot between each. Divide each side of tier into thirds at the top edge. Drop triple tube 3 strings from point to point. Add tube 15 top shell border and pipe a tube 3 bow at the intersections of the strings.

ADD FINISHING TOUCHES. Secure vase to top of cake with icing. Glue a pair of tiny bells to the top of each pillar and add a ribbon bow. Fill heart baskets on side of middle tier carefully with icing, then add snowdrops and leaves. The two lower tiers serve 148, the top tier serves an additional 18 guests.

The sweet-scented lily of the valley trims this bridal cake and its complementary groom's cake. This flower is one of the easiest to pipe, and a perfect trim for a spring wedding cake.

Decorate the bridal cake

PIPE FLOWERS AND LEAVES for top ornament. Pipe two long, curved tube 112 leaves on wax paper and dry. Curve 3" lengths of florists' wire and insert into a decorating bag fitted with tube 3 to coat with icing. Dry. Pipe flowers on the wires by making a tube 2 dot and pulling out four small points with the same tube for each tiny flower.

PREPARE TIERS. Bake 9" x 3" petal, 12" x 4" and 16" x 4" round tiers, each two layers. Fill and ice. Place base tier on a sturdy, 20" ruffle-edged, foil-covered board. Place middle tier on 14" plate and top tier on 10" plate from Crystal Clear Divider set. Assemble tiers as described on page 9.

DECORATE BASE TIER. Divide side of tier into eighths. At each division, pipe a pair of tube 112 leaves and three tube 3 stems. Pipe flowers on

stems by making a tube 2 dot and pulling out four small points with the same tube. Around base of tier, pipe tube 4B shells and trim each with a tube 104 ruffle. Circle top edge of tier with tube 16 shells. Divide top of tier into sixteenths, then pipe a tube 124 ruffled scallop from point to point. Edge scallops with tube 4 beading.

ON MIDDLE TIER, pipe tube 199 shells around base, then trim each with a tube 104 ruffle. Pipe a tube 4 curving vine around side of tier. Add tube 70 leaves and tube 3 stems on the vine. Pipe tube 2 flowers the same as for the base tier. Circle top edge of tier with tube 199 shells and trim each with a tube 4 string.

AT BASE OF TOP TIER, pipe tube 16 shells. Drop a string guideline on each petal on side of tier, pipe tube 124 ruffled scallop and edge scallop with tube 4 beading. On each petal pipe a tube 112 leaf, a tube 3 stem and flowers piped with tube 2 as described for base tier. Edge top of tier with tube 16 shells, then pipe tube 124 ruffled scallops on top of tier following the shape of the petals.

ADD FINISHING TOUCHES. Secure piped leaves and wired flowers to Kissing Lovebirds ornament with small mounds of icing. Attach ornament to top of cake. Pipe tube 14 shells around the base of each pillar, then attach a pair of small plastic doves at each of the lower pillars and a pair within the upper pillars. Two lower tiers serve 186 wedding guests, top tier serves 20.

Decorate the groom's cake

Bake a 10" x 4" square, two-layer cake. Fill and ice smoothly. Pipe tube 16 base shell border. Starting 1" from each corner, divide each side of the cake into thirds. Drop a string guideline, then pipe tube 17 zigzag garlands around cake and add tube 17 rosettes at the intersections. Lightly mark a 7" square on top of cake and outline with tube 17 "C"-shaped scrolls. Add a top rosette border with the same tube. In center of cake top, pipe long curved tube 113 leaves, then add curved tube 4 stems. Pipe lily of the valley flowers by piping tube 4 dots and pulling out four points from each with tube 2. Tie the bouquet with a tube 1 lovers knot. Serves wedding cake-size pieces to 50.

Spring, the time of new life and growing things, is a perfect time for a wedding—and daffodils bring a sunny spring glow to these lovely cakes.

The daffodil bridal cake

MAKE FLOWERS. Make about 45 royal icing daffodils in advance. Using tube 124 and a flower nail, pipe six separate petals. Pinch petals to a point with fingers dipped in cornstarch. Pipe center cup with tube 3, pressing out a coil of string, then add a tube 1 zigzag at the top. Dry some flat and others within a curved surface. Mount all but 24 daffodils on wire stems, then wrap wires with floral tape. Pipe spikes on the backs of the remaining flowers. (See page 14.) Make about 18 leaves. Curve 7″ lengths of florists' wire and insert into bag fitted with tube 68. Squeeze bag while removing wire. Push exposed wire into styrofoam to dry.

BAKE TWO-LAYER TIERS—16″ x 4″, 12″ x 4″ and 8″ x 3″ round. Fill and ice. Secure 16″ tier to a 20″ foil-covered board. Press tier with a 14″ round separator plate to mark position of pillars. Place a 5″ Corinthian pillar at each mark, then push a long dowel rod through pillars down to board beneath tier. Lift dowel and clip off ⅞″ below top of pillar. Push dowel back down. Set middle tier on a 14″ separator plate and assemble with top tier.

DECORATE BOTTOM TIER. Tape wired leaves and about ten wired daffodils into a bouquet. Bend the stems at a right angle and secure between the pillars with icing. Pipe double tube 13 scallops on the top of the tier from pillar to pillar. Add rosettes where scallops meet. Divide the side of the tier into sixteenths. In center of each division, drop triple tube 16 strings, leaving open space between each set. Pipe tube 18 top shell border. In the open spaces between strings, pipe three tube 5 stems and add tube 66 leaves. Secure spiked daffodils to tops of stems. Create bottom border with tube 4B shells, and trim each with a tube 70 leaf.

DECORATE MIDDLE TIER. Divide side of tier into twelfths. Drop triple tube 15 strings from point to point, letting every other set hang deeper. Below shallow strings, pipe a fan-like cluster of tube 68 leaves. Pipe shell borders, tube 18 on bottom, tube 16 on top. On the top of the tier at each division, pipe a tube 17 fleur-de-lis.

ON TOP TIER, pipe tube 16 bottom shell border. Divide side of tier into sixteenths. Drop tube 14 strings from point to point. At each intersection, pipe a tube 17 shell and star. Pipe top border with tube 16. Secure Petite Diamond Crown ornament to top of cake with icing, then arrange wired daffodils and leaves around the ornament. Two lower tiers serve 186 wedding guests, top tier serves 30.

The companion groom's cake

Pipe about 20 daffodils and dry within a curved surface. Pipe spikes on backs of 16 flowers.

Bake a 9″ x 13″ x 4″ two-layer sheet cake in the groom's favorite flavor. Fill and ice smoothly. Set on a 13″ x 17″ cake board. Using tube 18, pipe comma shapes and stars to create the base border. On the long sides, drop tube 13 triple strings, then pipe double strings on either side of it. On the short sides, pipe double strings in the center. Curve tube 13 stars below strings. Pipe tube 16 top shell border. Lightly mark a 7″ x 4½″ rectangle on the top of the cake. Pipe the design with tube 16, making "C's" and shells.

Pipe tube 4 stems at corners of cake and in top rectangle. Add tube 112 leaves. Attach daffodils on small mounds of icing on top of cake. Push in spiked flowers on sides. Cake serves 54.

There never was such a cake! Colorful, just-like-real tulips bloom on snowy tiers trimmed with sunshine yellow. The bride will always treasure the vision of this spectacular masterpiece.

Make the gum paste tulips first

Use the Flower Garden Cutter Set and make about 21 tulips on 8″ to 10″ stems, and 30 tulip leaves. Follow the directions in the instruction booklet that accompanies the cutters. You'll be delighted at how quickly and easily the flowers are created.

Bind four tulips and five leaves into a cluster with floral tape. You will need four of these clusters. The rest of the flowers and leaves will adorn the top tier and frame the ornament.

Decorate Spring Glory

Once the tulips are made, the cake is very easy and quick to decorate. The simple piped trims set off the lovely flowers.

PREPARE THE TIERS. Bake 18″ x 4″ square, 12″ x 4″ round and 8″ x 3″ round, two-layer tiers. Fill and ice. Assemble the cake on a 22″ square cake board using 12″ round separator plates and 5″ Corinthian pillars to raise the upper tiers.

DECORATE BASE TIER. Divide each side of tier into fifths. Within each section, mark design with a pattern press, then pipe with tube 16. At each marked point, pipe a tube 4B upright shell, extending about halfway up the side. Top shells with tube 18 stars. Complete the bottom border with tube 18 rosettes. Edge the lower separator plate with tube 18. On top of tier, mark scallops using side designs as a guide. Pipe feathered scallops with tube 16. Pipe tube 18 top shell border. Glue a ribbon bow to the top of a 4″ plastic filigree heart. Glue heart on separator plate and attach two 2½″ White Birds in front of it.

DIVIDE SIDE OF MIDDLE TIER into sixteenths. At each division, pipe a tube 32 upright shell beginning at the base of the tier. Top each with a tube 18 star. Pipe tube 18 rosettes between the shells. On the top edge of the tier, drop tube 14 double strings from point to point. Add tube 16 rosettes and pipe tube 16 top shell border.

ON TOP TIER, pipe tube 4B upright shells, beginning at the top edge of tier and moving down for a crown effect. Add tube 18 stars. Pipe tube 16 shells around base of tier. Using the lower points of the upright shells as a guide, drop tube 14 strings from

point to point. Pipe a tube 16 star at each point. For top ornament, glue a 7″ plastic filigree heart to a Heart Base, then glue Bridal Couple in front of the heart. Dry, then secure ornament to top of tier.

ARRANGE FLOWERS. Insert two Flower Spikes into the top tier behind the ornament. Arrange tulips and leaves in the spikes letting most of the flowers extend out through the filigree heart.

For the clusters on the base tier, turn four Petite Heart Bases (without top plate) upside down to form bowls and set close to each pillar. Secure with icing. Push a Flower Spike into the tier in the center of each bowl. Pipe a little icing into spikes and insert prepared clusters of tulips and leaves.

The gum paste tulips can be carefully removed from the cake before it is served and inserted into a vase that has a piece of styrofoam secured in it. This makes a lovely memento for the bride and the spectacular flowers will remain beautiful and life-like for many years to come!

Without the 30-serving top tier, Spring Glory serves 230 wedding guests.

Elegant in its construction and feminine in its dainty, flowery trim, Apple Blossom is designed for a formal wedding reception. Little twin cakes, iced in palest pink, are gifts for the parents of the bride and the groom.

Decorate the bridal cake

MAKE FLOWERS FIRST. Pipe many, many small apple blossoms with five identically shaped, rounded petals. Use tube 101 and tube 101s for two sizes. Pipe small dots for stamens with tube 1. Set aside to dry.

PREPARE THE THREE-LAYER TIERS. Base tier consists of two 16″ round layers, each 2″ high, topped by a 16″ layer baked in the 16″ base bevel pan. Middle tier is two 12″ round layers, each 1½″ high, topped by a third layer baked in the 12″ top bevel pan. Top tier is constructed of two 8″ round layers, each 1½″ high and one layer baked in the 8″ top bevel pan. Fill and ice the tiers.

Assemble the cake in the following way. Secure the 16″ tier to a 20″ round, ruffle-edged cake board. Insert a circle of twelve dowels, clipped off level with top. (See page 8.) Push a 12″ round separator plate (from Crystal Clear pillar set) down into the top of the tier with the studs for the pillars down. Be sure the plate is flat against the surface of the cake. This plate takes the place of the cardboard cake circle which is usually placed in this position to provide extra support for the heavy tiers above.

Secure the 12″ tier on top of the separator plate. Use a 9″ separator plate to mark position of pillars on top of this tier. Set pillars in place and push a dowel rod through each, down to separator plate below tier. Pull up and clip off ⅞″ shorter than pillars, then push down again.

Secure top tier to 9″ separator plate, then place tier in position on pillars.

DECORATE THE BASE TIER FIRST. Pipe tube 4B shells around bottom of tier. Trim each shell with a tube 3 string and pipe a dot at points of string. Divide the side of the tier into twenty-fourths, marking about 1″ below edge of bevel. Drop tube 2 strings from the marks. Drop a second row of strings ½″ below, then a third row for triple scallops. Add a tube 2 dot at each intersection. Pipe tube 16 shell border around top edge of tier.

ON THE MIDDLE TIER, divide the side of the tier into sixteenths, marking about ¾″ below edge of bevel. Drop three rows of tube 2 strings just as you did for the base tier. Add tube 2 dots. Pipe tube 16 shell borders around base and top of tier and around the edge of the separator plate.

DIVIDE SIDE OF TOP TIER into twelfths along the top edge. Drop double tube 2 strings from point to point. Pipe tube 18 shells around base of tier, tube 16 shells around the top and edge of the bevel.

ADD FINISHING TOUCHES. Glue two small doves to a 4″ plastic Filigree Heart and dry. Secure between the pillars, attach apple blossoms and pipe tube 65 leaves. Secure top ornament to cake with icing, and trim with flowers and leaves. Attach apple blossoms to the bevel on each of the three tiers with dots of icing. Around the base of the top tier, secure eight small clusters of flowers, using pillars as guide. Trim flowers with tube 65 leaves. The two lower tiers serve a total of 186, the top tier serves an additional 30 guests.

Decorate the parents' cakes

These two little cakes are made especially with the parents of the bride and the groom in mind. Bake the layers in their favorite flavors or add a special filling just for them.

Make apple blossoms for the cakes the same as for the bridal cake. For each cake, bake an 8″ x 2″ layer and an 8″ top bevel. Fill and ice. Secure each cake to a 12″ ruffle-edged cake board. Pipe tube 9 bottom ball border, adding tube 4 dots. Divide the side of the cake into twelfths and mark about ¾″ below edge of bevel. Drop three rows of tube 2 strings, just as you did for base tier of bridal cake. Add tube 2 dots. Pipe a tube 4 border around the top and the edge of the bevel.

Secure a seated cherub in the center of one cake, a standing cherub in the center of the other. Trim the cherubs with apple blossoms, attaching with icing. Complete the cakes by covering bevel area with flowers, attaching with dots of icing. Trim with tube 65 leaves. Each cake provides ten generous dessert-size servings.

Flowers in fresh pastels, exuberant cupids, and graceful trim make Love's Fantasy a perfect centerpiece for a happy celebration.

Decorate the bridal cake

MAKE FLOWERS FIRST. Pipe many wild roses using tubes 104 and 124 and royal icing. Add tube 2 centers. Dry within a curved surface. To make the center ornament on base tier, roll parchment paper into a cone, cut off the tip so the cone stands 4″ high. Pipe lines of icing down the cone and attach the wild roses. Add tube 66 leaves. Dry.

PREPARE TIERS. Bake 16″ x 4″, 12″ x 4″ and 8″ x 3″ round, two-layer tiers. Fill and ice. Assemble on a 20″ foil-covered cake board using a pair of 14″ round separator plates and 5″ Corinthian pillars to elevate the 12″ tier. Raise the 8″ tier with 10″ separator plates and 5″ Corinthian pillars. When assembling the cake, secure cone covered with flowers between the lower pillars and Adoration ornament between the upper pillars.

ON BOTTOM TIER, pipe a tube 4B bottom star border. Drop a tube 3 string over the stars. Divide the top edge of the tier into sixteenths. Drop a tube 5 string guideline from point to point. Then pipe over the guideline with the same tube and a circular motion. Drop four tube 4 strings from point to point. Mark scallops on the top of tier using a 3¼″ round cutter. Pipe lattice within the scallops with tube 2. Pipe around the edge of the scallop with tube 3 and a circular motion. Pipe top reverse shell border on tier with tube 14.

DECORATE THE MIDDLE TIER the same as the bottom tier using the same tubes. Use a 2½″ round cutter to mark the scallops on the top of the tier.

ON THE TOP TIER, pipe tube 21 bottom star border. Trim stars with tube 2 strings. Pipe tube 14 reverse shell top border. Pipe tube 2 curved vine on side of tier and add leaves with tube 65. Attach flowers to vine with dots of icing.

ADD FINISHING TOUCHES. Secure seated cherubs at edge of lower 14″ separator plate. Attach flowers around cherubs with icing, extending them down side of tier. On side of middle tier, attach flowers between every second scallop. Secure standing cherub to top of cake and attach flowers around it. Trim all flowers with tube 66 leaves. Top tier serves 30, two lower tiers serve 186 guests.

The Fantasy shower cake

Colorful wild roses and a happy cherub add to the joyful mood of this shower cake. It's a pretty little preview of the bridal cake.

MAKE FLOWER TRIMS. Pipe five-petalled wild roses with tube 104 and royal icing. Add tube 2 centers and dry within a curved surface.

DECORATE CAKE. Bake a 9″ x 13″ two-layer sheet cake. Fill and ice. Pipe tube 8 bulb border around base of cake. Divide the long sides of the cake into fourths and the short sides into thirds, starting 1¼″ in from each corner. Drop a string guideline from point to point, then pipe tube 7 circular-motion garlands following the guideline. Add tube 3 strings and a little twirl at each point. Pipe a tube 4 curving vine around the side of the cake. Attach wild roses and pipe tube 67 leaves.

Transfer Beautiful Bridal pattern to top of cake. Write the couple's names on front center of oval, then complete with scallops and tube 2. Pipe vine with tube 4. Attach flowers and pipe tube 67 leaves. Edge top of tier with tube 16 reverse shells. Secure cherub from Cherub Concerto set within the oval, attach flowers at its base and pipe tube 67 leaves. The cake serves dessert-size pieces to 24.

An exquisite cake for a joyful occasion! Satiny rolled fondant covers the tiers and sets off the airy trim and delicate flowers.

Decorate the bridal cake

PIPE FLOWERS. Pipe many daisies with royal icing in two sizes using tubes 124 and 104. Pipe tube 6 centers and flatten with finger dipped in tinted granulated sugar. Dry within a curved surface.

PREPARE TIERS. Bake 16" x 4", 12" x 4" and 8" x 4" round, two-layer tiers using a firm pound cake recipe. Fill the layers, then cover the tiers with marzipan and rolled fondant as described on page 109. Place the base tier on a 20" round cake board, middle tier on a 12" separator plate and top tier on an 8" separator plate. Mark the position of the pillars on the base tier with a 12" separator plate and on the middle tier with an 8" separator plate. Pin Beautiful Bridal patterns on tiers and trace with a pin. Remove patterns. Mark designs with pattern press on top of base tier within pattern sections and on lower edge of middle and top tiers between pattern sections.

DECORATE BASE TIER. Along the bottom border, divide the areas between the sections of the pattern in half. Pipe tube 13 guidelines from the center points of the pattern sections to the marked points between them. Pipe over guideline using tube 14 and a circling motion. Pipe over pattern lines with tube 13, and a circling motion.

Attach daisies to Lovenest ornament then secure in center of tier. Surround with daisies. Set pillars in marked position, then push dowel rods through them to cake board. Lift dowel rods, clip off at a point ⅞" below top of pillars and push back again to touch cake board.

ON MIDDLE TIER, pipe over pattern lines with tube 13, using a tight circling motion. Secure Cherub Concerto figure in center of tier and surround with daisies. Attach pillars the same as for base tier. Now set tier in position on pillars of base tier. For bottom border, pipe curved garlands with tube 13 and circling motion. Add tube 67 leaves, points extending below tier.

ON TOP TIER, pipe over pattern lines with tube 13 and a tight circling motion. Place tier in position on the pillars below. Pipe bottom border the same as for the middle tier. Trim Springtime Love ornament with daisies, set on top of tier and edge the base with tube 6.

ADD FINISHING TOUCHES. Pipe freehand flower stems on bottom tier with tube 2. Attach daisies to stems with dots of icing and pipe leaves with tube 65. Use thinned icing for a perky look. Add flower trim to the two upper tiers the same way. If the bride plans to freeze the 30-serving top tier, two lower tiers will serve 186 guests.

HOW TO CARRY. Remove top tier with pillars and attach to an 8" separator plate. Follow the same procedure for the middle tier using a 12" separator plate. This will prevent the bottom trim of the tiers from getting broken. Transport the tiers in depressions in pieces of foam rubber as usual (see page 125). Re-assemble the cake at the reception and trim bases of all pillars with daisies.

The Festival shower cake

Pipe daisies the same as for the bridal cake. Bake a 12" round, two-layer pound cake. Cover with marzipan and rolled fondant as described on page 109. Pipe tube 16 shells around base. Divide side of cake into eighths and mark designs with a pattern press, then pipe with tube 13 and "C" motions. Pipe two tube 16 circular motion garlands between each design. Trace Beautiful Bridal pattern on top of cake, then pipe with tube 13 and "C" motions. Secure Kneeling Cherub Fountain in center and insert Parasol Picks around it. Trim picks and fountain with flowers. Add daisy clusters to sides of cake and trim all flowers with tube 66 leaves. Serves generous, dessert-size pieces to 22 guests.

Sweet-faced pansies are a charming accent on a summer wedding cake. The cake itself is simple and quick to decorate.

Decorate the wedding cake

MAKE FLOWERS. Pipe pansies with royal icing in three pastels, using tube 124. Pipe the four small, overlapping upper petals in a semi-circle. Then pipe the large, lower, ruffled petal and add center with tube 2. Dry within a large curved surface. Paint in the flower "faces" with a small artist's brush and food coloring. Pipe a royal icing spike on the backs of about 32 pansies. (See page 14.)

BAKE AND ICE TIERS. Bake 16" x 4", 12" x 4" and 8" x 3" round, two-layer tiers. Fill and ice smoothly. Assemble the cake on a 20" ruffle-edged cake board. Use 14" round separator plates and 7½" Corinthian pillars to raise the middle tier. Use 10" plates and 5" Corinthian pillars to raise the top tier.

DECORATE TIERS. Pipe tube 22 shells around bottom of base tier. Divide top edge of tier into eighths and drop tube 14 triple strings from point to point. Fill area below strings with tube 14 spaced stars. Edge separator plate with tube 18, then pipe tube 20 shells around top edge of tier.

On the middle tier, pipe tube 16 shells around bottom of tier. Divide top edge of tier into eighths, then drop tube 14 triple strings from point to point. Fill area below strings with tube 14 spaced stars. Edge separator plate on top of tier with tube 17. Add tube 19 top shell border.

Pipe tube 18 shells around base of top tier. Divide top edge of tier into eighths and pipe tube 14 double strings. Below strings pipe spaced tube 14 stars. Add a tube 17 top shell border.

ADD FINISHING TOUCHES. Create bell ornament to set between the lower pillars. Glue a 2¾" x 2½" plastic Filigree Bell to top plate of Petite Heart Base. Glue three more bells of the same size to the top of the first so open edges of bells rest on the plate. Dry, then attach pansies to the bells with dots of icing. Secure between the lower pillars. Push in spiked pansies between the strings on the base and middle tiers. Secure Angel Fountain between the upper pillars and add flowers. Top the cake with Petite Heavenly Bells ornament and attach pansies. Add tube 66 leaves to all the flowers. Top tier serves 30, two lower tiers serve 186 guests.

Decorate the cake for the groom

The tradition of the groom's cake is popular once again. Here is an especially handsome one, covered with mocha buttercream and trimmed with a cascade of pansies in deep rich colors.

Pipe the pansies, then add royal icing spikes on the backs of ten flowers.

Bake a 12" x 4" round, two-layer cake. Fill and ice. Place cake on a 16" cake board or tray. Mark vertical lines on side of cake, using a small triangle. Now cover side with tube 1D stripes, using marked lines to keep stripes vertical. Pipe tube 22 bottom star border and tube 22 top shell border. Secure pansies to the cake in a cascade with dots of icing. Use spiked flowers on side. Add tube 67 leaves. The cake provides 68 wedding-sized servings.

Here's a cake as bright as a sunny summer day with a garden of flowers adorning its tiers. It's perfect for an outdoor reception, just as pretty indoors.

PIPE ROYAL ICING FLOWERS. Make many daisies with tubes 103 and 104. Attach a square of wax paper to a flower nail with a dot of icing. Pipe a small icing dot in the middle to keep the petals centered. Touch the wide end of the tube to the outer edge of the nail and press out the icing, moving in to the center dot. Lighten the pressure so the petal narrows at the base. Repeat around the nail for a full circle of petals. Pipe center with tube 8 and flatten with a damp fingertip dipped in yellow-tinted granulated sugar. Slide paper off to dry daisies within and over a curved surface.

Pipe many tube 104 wild roses. Attach wax paper square to a flower nail. Beginning at the center of the nail, press out the first petal, curving slightly upward at the edge to form a cupped shape. Pipe four more petals the same way, then add tube 2 dots for the stamens in the center.

Make many bachelor's buttons by piping a tube 6 mound of pale blue icing on a wax paper square secured to a flower nail with icing. Pipe a cluster of tube 1 dots on top of the mound. With tube 14 and deeper blue icing, pull out tiny star petals around the center dots and cover the rest of the mound. Add more petals here and there for a full fluffy flower. Slide paper off to dry thoroughly.

Mount all of the flowers on wire stems (see page 14). Pipe tube 65 leaves on wires and dry.

Tape flowers and leaves together into a nosegay for the top of the cake. To form a holder, cut a wedge from a 4¾" paper circle and tape into a cone. Cut off the tip so the stems can go through. For the lacy edge, cut paper doilies, ruffle them and tape inside the cone. Insert the flowers and tie with a ribbon bow. Bind the remaining flowers and leaves into twelve small clusters with floral tape. (These make pretty keepsakes for the bridesmaids after the cake is served.)

PREPARE THE ROUND TIERS. Base tier is 16" x 4", two layers. Middle tier is a 12" single layer. Top tier is 8" x 3", two layers. Ice and assemble on a 20" ruffled-edged cake board. Insert dowel supports into the two lower tiers as shown on page 8. Use 10" round separator plates and 5" Grecian pillars below the 8" top tier.

DECORATE THE CAKE. On the 16" tier, pipe shell borders using tube 19 around the bottom and tube 17 around the top. On the side of the tier, trace "S"-shaped scroll design with a toothpick, then pipe with tube 16. Over-pipe with the same tube. On the 12" tier, pipe tube 16 bottom shell border and tube 15 top shell border. Edge lower separator plate with tube 14.

On 8" tier, pipe tube 14 bottom shell border and tube 13 top shell border. On the side of tier, pipe scroll design similar to base tier, but use tube 14 to pipe and over-pipe the scrolls.

ADD ORNAMENT AND FLOWERS. Glue Petite Bridal Couple to Petite Heart Base and secure between the pillars with icing. Arrange two clusters of flowers on either side of the bridal couple. Push ten Flower Spikes, evenly spaced, into the top of the 16" tier. Insert a cluster of flowers into each spike to form a wreath. Set nosegay on top of cake. The two lower tiers serve 152 guests, top tier 30.

A profusion of tiny flowers, bright as a rainbow after a gentle summer shower, bloom on this colorful bridal cake.

Decorate the bridal cake

PIPE MANY DROP FLOWERS using tubes 35, 190 and 225. Add tube 2 centers. Dry, then mount about half on wire stems. Pipe tube 65 leaves on wires. Tape into four large sprays and six clusters.

PREPARE WREATH. Using round cutters, cut a 4" circle from gum paste (recipe on page 128) and remove a 3" circle from the center. Dry flat. Bend a 20" length of florists' wire into a circle so 5" of each end of wire extends from bottom. Twist these ends together, then secure wire to back of wreath with royal icing. Cut another gum paste circle the same as the first. Brush back of dried wreath with egg white and press wet gum paste piece to it. Dry thoroughly. Secure flowers around wreath, then pipe tube 65 royal icing leaves.

PREPARE TIERS. Bake 16" x 4" square, 10" x 4" round and 6" x 3" round, two-layer tiers. Fill and ice. Assemble cake on a 20" square foil-covered board using 12" round separator plates and 5" Grecian pillars with Snap-On Filigree.

DECORATE TIERS. For the bottom border on base tier, pipe tube 4B shells, then frame each with tube 104. Add ruffles between shells with same tube. Edge the separator plate with tube 18. For top border, pipe tube 32 shells.

On middle tier, pipe bottom border the same as on base tier. Pipe tube 18 reverse shell top border.

On top tier, pipe tube 18 bottom shell border and tube 17 reverse shell top border.

ADD FLOWERS AND ORNAMENT. On the bottom tier, push a Flower Spike into the tier close to the corner of each pillar. Insert one of the large sprays into each of the spikes. Secure drop flowers in cascades near each corner (see page 10). Add tube 65 leaves. Attach a Musical Trio cherub between each pair of pillars with royal icing.

Push six Flower Spikes, evenly spaced, into the top of the middle tier and insert a cluster of flowers into each to create a garland effect.

Glue Petite Bridal Couple to Petite Heart Base. Make a hole in the base behind couple with a heated ice pick or nail. Secure ornament with icing, then push wire on wreath through hole and down into cake. Attach a few drop flowers to base of ornament and add tube 65 leaves. Two lower tiers serve 176 guests, top tier serves 16.

The shower cake is a bridesmaid

DECORATE DOLL. Bake skirt in Wonder Mold pan. Ice with a thin coat of buttercream icing, then insert Little Girl Pick into top. Mark eight scallops around skirt. Pipe tube 16 stars below the scallops, then pipe three rows of tube 104 ruffles, following the scallop design. Cover skirt and bodice with tube 16 stars. Pipe a double row of tube 101 ruffles around neckline and edge top with tube 1 beading. Attach drop flowers made with tubes 35, 190 and 225 above and below bottom ruffles and pipe tube 65 leaves. Secure a small ribbon bow at waist.

DECORATE PARASOL. Trim the top of a Party Parasol with drop flowers, securing with dots of royal icing. Pipe tube 65 leaves. Attach a ribbon bow to the top of the parasol, another to the handle. Wire the parasol handle to doll's hand. Serves twelve dessert-size portions.

This fascinating cake is trimmed with dainty embroidery and the traditional bride's flower—but its construction is new and unique. An easy-to-serve sheet cake is topped by a small square tier.

PIPE ORANGE BLOSSOMS. Cover an indented, saucer-shaped flower nail with foil. Pipe five tube 81 petals in a circle on the nail and pinch each to a point with fingers dusted with cornstarch. Then pipe two upright petals with tube 81 in the center to form a cup. Dry, then pipe tube 1 dots around the top edge of the cup. Pipe royal icing spikes on the backs of about half the flowers with tube 5.

PREPARE THE TIERS. Bake a 12″ x 18″ x 4″ two-layer rectangle and an 8″ x 3″ two-layer square tier. Fill and ice. Place base tier on a 16″ x 22″ ruffle-edged cake board. Mark position of 8″ upper tier—2″ in from one short side of rectangle and 2″ from both long sides. Insert dowels in base tier for support, then set upper tier in place. Lightly mark a rectangle on top of base tier, using top tier as one end, and measuring 2″ in from opposite short side. Measuring 1″ in from each corner of marked rectangle, divide long sides into eighths, short sides into fourths. Pipe tube 3 scallops from point to point. Add a tube 3 dot at the intersections.

DECORATE THE BASE TIER. Pipe tube 21 star border around the bottom of the tier. Divide the top edge of the tier into eighths on the short sides and into twelfths on the long sides. Drop a tube 3 string from point to point around the tier. Trim the sides of the tier with tube 2 embroidery. Pipe five-petalled flowers, beginning with a center dot and pulling each of the petals from the center out. Pipe a flower within each scallop on the top of the tier. Edge top of tier with tube 19 star border.

DECORATE THE UPPER TIER. Pipe tube 18 star border around the bottom of the tier. Divide each side of the tier into sixths along the top edge. Drop a tube 3 string from point to point. Trim the sides of the tier with embroidery, done just as on base tier. Edge top of tier with tube 18 star border. Secure ornament to the top of the tier with icing, then pipe tube 3 scallops around the ornament base.

Position orange blossoms in a graceful cascade from the ornament to the base of the cake. Use spiked flowers on tier sides. Add tube 67 leaves to the flowers. The base tier serves 108 guests and the top tier an additional 32.

The daintiest, laciest shower cake

Using your own patterns, make one 5″ heart and four 2¼″ hearts with Color Flow technique and dry. Add tube 2 lettering. Pipe a royal icing spike on back of each small heart. Pipe tube 1s lace pieces on wax paper, using Beautiful Bridal patterns. Make royal icing drop flowers with tubes 26 and 35. Add tube 2 centers and dry.

Bake an 8″ x 4″ square, two-layer cake. Fill, ice and place on a 12″ cake board. Pipe tube 5 bottom bead border. Add tube 3 beading around top of cake and down the corners. Divide each side of cake into fifths and drop a tube 5 string from point to point. Over-pipe the string with tube 3, then tube 2. Pipe hearts at the intersections of the over-piped strings with tube 3. Attach a small Color Flow heart to each side of cake, pushing in spike on a mound of icing. Attach large heart on top on mounds of icing, lifting on sugar cubes at rear. Secure lace pieces to edges of hearts with royal icing, holding in position until icing sets. Add tube 2 beading. Attach drop flowers and trim with tube 65 leaves. Cake provides twelve dessert-size servings.

A cake as young and carefree as a summer breeze! Fluffy daisies pave the sunny tiers, framed by simple white borders. Daisy Field is very easy to decorate, but its effect is spectacular. Pipe the flowers well in advance and the decorating will go quickly.

Decorate the wedding cake

PIPE THE FLOWERS. Make many tubes 103 and 104 royal icing daisies on squares of wax paper, secured to a flower nail with a dab of icing. Pipe centers with tube 4 and flatten with a fingertip dipped in tinted granulated sugar. Pipe a few more for the ornament trim with tubes 101 and 101s and add tube 2 centers. Dry within a curved surface. When thoroughly dry, carefully peel the wax paper from the backs of the flowers.

PREPARE THE TIERS. Bake 14″ x 3″, 10″ x 3″ and 6″ x 3″ round, two-layer tiers. Fill and ice tiers. Daisy Field is constructed on the Lace Cake Stand. Glue legs to the 16″ plate. Follow the directions on page 9 for preparing and assembling the tiers. Set the 14″ tier on the 16″ plate and the 10″ tier on a 12″

plate. Use an 8″ plate for the top 6″ tier.

DECORATE THE CAKE. Beginning with the 14″ bottom tier, pipe tube 4B base shell border. Outline shells with tube 74 scallops. Add curves of tube 2 dots above the shells. Pipe tube 16 top shell border. Cover the entire top surface of the tier with daisies, tilting each on a small mound of icing.

On middle tier, pipe a tube 32 bottom shell border and outline the shells with tube 76 scallops. Add curves of tube 2 dots above the shells. Top shell border is piped with tube 16. Now pave the top of the tier with daisies, just as you did on base tier, tilting each on a small mound of icing.

On the top tier, pipe tube 32 bottom shell border. Outline each shell with tube 76 scallops. Add curves of tube 2 dots above the shells. Secure Petite Double Ring ornament to the top of the tier and trim with the two smallest sizes of daisies. Cover remaining top surface of the tier with daisies, using all four sizes. Set each on a mound of icing. If the bride plans to freeze the 16-serving top tier for the first anniversary, the two lower tiers serve 140 wedding guests.

Serve daisy petits fours at a shower

Everyone will love these dainty, delicious little cakes—and they make such a festive appearance on the table. Prepare them several days ahead of the party if you like. The poured fondant covering keeps the cakes fresh and moist.

Pipe daisies with royal icing using tube 103. Pipe centers with tube 4 and flatten with a fingertip dipped in yellow-tinted granulated sugar. Dry within a curved surface.

Bake a cake in a sheet cake pan, 1″ high. Cut in two and fill and stack the two halves, using buttercream or jam. Cut the filled cake into 2″ strips, then diagonally into diamonds. Ice each with white buttercream, then set on a rack and cover with tinted poured fondant. (See pages 127 and 128 for recipe and directions for pouring.)

After the fondant has set, decorate the petits fours. Pipe a tube 3 curved stem on each and add tube 65 leaves. Secure a daisy at the top of the stem on a dot of icing.

59

Gracefully proportioned and heaped with old-fashioned sweet peas, the pale pink tiers are softened by snowy cornelli lace.

Decorate the wedding cake

PIPE ROYAL ICING SWEET PEAS in two shades of pink (see page 10). Use tubes 101, 103 and 104. Dry.

BAKE THE TIERS, 14" x 4" square, 10" x 4" round and 6" x 3" square, each two layers. Fill, ice and assemble on an 18", ruffle-edged cake board using 7" square separator plates and 5" Grecian pillars.

DECORATE TWO LOWER TIERS. Cut a scallop pattern 9" wide, 3" deep for sides of base tier. Cut a second pattern for corners on top of tier. Measure circumference of middle tier with a strip of paper and divide in fourths. Using this measurement for width, cut a 2½" deep scallop pattern for side of middle tier. Trace patterns on tiers.

Fill marked areas on both tiers with tube 1 cornelli lace. Edge scallops with tube 2 beading and add tube 3 fleurs-de-lis at points. Pipe tube 8 ball border at base of bottom tier and tube 7 border on top edge, up to cornelli area. Circle base of middle tier with tube 7 and pipe top border with tube 6. Use same tube to edge separator plate.

ON TOP TIER, drop string guidelines to mark four scallops on each side of tier. Fill area from scallops to bottom of tier with tube 1 cornelli lace. Edge scallops with tube 2 beading and add fleurs-de-lis at points. Pipe ball border at base with tube 6, at top of tier with tube 5.

FINISH THE TRIM. Gather a 12" strip of tulle, 2" wide, to make a pouf. Attach to center of separator plate with royal icing, then set a Musical Trio cherub on the pouf. Remove artificial flowers from Enchantment ornament and replace with piped sweet peas, attaching with royal icing. Set ornament on top of cake, securing with icing.

Now add the fluffy flower cascades on all three tiers, just as shown on page 10. Create miniature cascades on base of each corner of the top tier. Pink Perfection is complete—and pretty as its picture! Two lower tiers serve 146, the top tier 16.

A pretty pink shower cake

All the girls will be thrilled with this party centerpiece! To trim it, you will need sweet peas piped with tubes 101, 103 and 104.

MAKE GUM PASTE PARASOL. Make gum paste using recipe on page 128. Roll out 1/16" thick, cut out, follow Beautiful Bridal pattern, and dry on a 4"

Ball Mold dusted with cornstarch. Then remove the mold and pipe tube 1 cornelli lace inside the parasol. For handle, paint a 4½" length of ¼" dowel rod with thinned royal icing and dry. Secure the handle to the inside of the parasol with royal icing and dry. Roll a ¼" diameter cylinder of gum paste and attach to top of parasol with egg white. Dry. Pipe a tube 102 ruffle around the edge, then add tube 2 beading. Trim with tube 101 sweet peas and a ribbon bow.

DECORATE THE CAKE. Bake a 10" square, two-layer cake. Fill, ice and place on ruffle-edged cake board. Cut a scallop pattern 2½" deep, 8" wide for cake sides. Fold an 8" paper circle in eighths and cut scallop pattern for cake top. Trace patterns on cake with toothpick. Now decorate, using tube 1 for cornelli, tube 2 for beading and tubes 8 and 5 for base border. Pipe top border with tube 6 and message with tube 2. Insert handle of parasol and trim cake with sweet peas on mounds of icing. Serves 20 dessert-size portions.

Radiant marigolds climb toward the sky on this summer bridal cake. Despite its opulent appearance, Sunshine is easy to decorate.

How to decorate Sunshine

MAKE FLUFFY MARIGOLDS AHEAD. Use a flower nail with a square of wax paper secured on top, tube 104 and royal icing. Pipe a circle of ruffled petals, lifting them slightly at the tips. Repeat for two more rows of petals, making each shorter than the last. Fill center with petals that stand almost straight up. Pipe smaller marigolds with tubes 101 and 102. Pipe tube 65 ruffled leaves on wires. Dry, then tape stems together into many sprays.

BAKE TIERS. Bake 14″ x 4″ square, 12″ x 4″ round and 8″ x 4″ round, two-layer tiers. Fill and ice. Assemble on an 18″ ruffle-edged cake board.

DECORATE TIERS. On each tier, pipe bottom shell borders with tube 32, top shell borders with tube 19. Use tube 16 for all tier-side trims. Divide each side of base tier into fifths and pipe a feathered "S" shape in each division. Divide middle tier into eighths and pipe facing "S" shapes. Do top tier same as base tier, first dividing into eighths. Insert four Stairsteps with candles into side of each tier in cascade effect. Secure marigolds to the stairsteps and on the tops of the tiers. Glue Bridal Couple to the Floral Scroll Base. Secure to top of cake, then add more marigolds. Trim flowers with leaf sprays and pipe a few more ruffled leaves with tube 65. Top tier serves 30, two lower tiers 166 guests.

Decorate the groom's cake

PIPE MARIGOLDS with tubes 104 and 102, the same as on wedding cake. Pipe other varieties with a single or double row of tube 101 petals, filling centers with tube 13 stars. Brush on accents with thinned paste colors. Prepare tube 65 leaf sprays.

BAKE, FILL AND ICE a 12″ x 4″ round, two-layer cake. Pipe twelve tube 3 stems on side of cake and add tube 65 leaves. Pipe tube 32 base border, tube 19 top border. Arrange the marigolds and leaf sprays on the cake, securing with icing. Add a few tube 65 leaves. Serves 68 wedding cake-size pieces.

This stately formal cake is just as radiant as a sunny fall day. Ribboned bridal bouquets cascade from each pillar, more flowers adorn the tiers.

PIPE CHRYSANTHEMUMS IN ADVANCE in royal icing. Here is a list of the flowers you'll need:

32 white flowers on wire stems for bouquets

52 unstemmed white flowers. Of these, pipe spikes on the backs of 42. (see page 14.)

62 gold flowers. Pipe spikes on the backs of 52

To pipe the stemmed white flowers, pipe a tube 10 ball of icing on the end of a 6″ length of florists' wire. Set in styrofoam to dry. Starting at the top of the ball, pipe a few upstanding tube 81 petals with yellow icing. Change to white icing and cover the ball with rows of tube 81 petals.

To pipe the unstemmed flowers, white and gold, pipe a tube 10 mound of icing on a number 7 flower nail. Beginning at base of mound, cover it with rows of 81 petals. For white flowers, use yellow icing for the last few petals at the top of the mound. Slide off nail to dry, then pipe spikes on backs of flowers as the list above indicates.

Pipe about 150 deeply lobed leaves in royal icing on a flower nail, using tube 104. Dry within a curved surface. Attach wire stems with dots of icing to the backs of about 30 of the leaves.

Make four bouquets of stemmed white chrysanthemums and leaves, taping stems together. Tie each with a fluffy bow.

BAKE TIERS—two 15″ x 3″ two-layer petals, a 12″ x 4″ two-layer round, an 8″ x 4″ two-layer round, a small Wonder Mold and a 6″ x 1″ layer. Cut a 3½″ circle from the 6″ x 1″ layer. Ice top and set small wonder mold on it, then ice all over. Fill all tiers, ice round tiers only. Ice the top of one 15″ petal tier. Cut a cardboard cake circle to the same size and shape as tier, wrap in clear plastic and lay on top of it. Now add second petal tier. This forms base tier. Ice smoothly and set on 20″ cake board. These tiers are separated before serving the cake and each is cut individually. Assemble cake with dowels, using 10″ separator plates and 7½″ Corinthian pillars.

DECORATE BASE TIER. Pipe a tube 18 bottom shell border. Drop string guidelines on each petal of the tier, then pipe tube 18 zigzag garlands. Trim each garland with four tube 2 strings. At the top edge of the tier, drop guidelines in center of each petal. Pipe three tube 17 zigzag garlands within guidelines, one above the other, right up to top edge of tier. Pipe smaller tube 16 garlands on either side. Trim all garlands with tube 2 strings

and loops. Pipe tube 16 top shell border.

DECORATE MIDDLE TIER. Pipe a tube 16 bottom shell border. Using pillars as guide, drop string guidelines for four large garlands on tier side. Pipe garlands with tube 17 zigzags. In the four spaces between the large garlands, drop triple guidelines for small garlands. Pipe with tube 16 zigzags. Trim all garlands with tube 2 strings and loops. Do top shell border and edge separator plate with tube 16.

ON THE TOP TIER, pipe a tube 16 bottom shell border. Drop eight guidelines around tier, using pillars as guide. Following guidelines, pipe tube 16 zigzag garlands. Trim with tube 2 strings and loops. Pipe a tube 16 top shell border.

DECORATE SMALL WONDER MOLD. Drop tube 2 strings around sides and trim with loops and fleurs-de-lis piped with same tube.

ADD FLOWERS. On the bottom tier, push in eight groups of spiked flowers as pictured. Attach leaves with icing. Glue Bridal Couple to Heart Base and secure between pillars with icing. Attach bouquets to each pillar with a florists' wire hook. Push spiked gold flowers into tier side below bouquets to give the effect of cascades. Circle the wonder mold with unspiked flowers, then add a group on top, securing all with icing. Tuck in leaves on dots of icing. The three lower tiers serve 192, top tier, including wonder mold, 32.

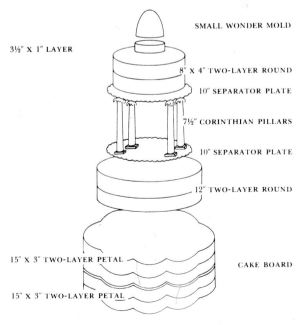

SMALL WONDER MOLD

3½″ x 1″ LAYER

8″ x 4″ TWO-LAYER ROUND

10″ SEPARATOR PLATE

7½″ CORINTHIAN PILLARS

10″ SEPARATOR PLATE

12″ TWO-LAYER ROUND

15″ x 3″ TWO-LAYER PETAL

CAKE BOARD

15″ x 3″ TWO-LAYER PETAL

SEPARATE TWO PETAL TIERS TO CUT INDIVIDUALLY

HOLIDAY. Decorating directions page 68

MISTLETOE.
Decorating directions page 68

What a happy time for a wedding! Every heart is filled with love, every face is smiling, the spirit of celebration is everywhere. It's a joyful task to trim a cake for a holiday reception!

Holiday *shown on page 66*

Cheerful holly, a glint of gilt and a Christmas tree on top—Holiday is as merry as the season.

MAKE HOLLY LEAVES. Make about 110 gum paste holly leaves using Flower Garden Cutters and instruction booklet. Mount about 24 leaves on wires and make three clusters of gum paste berries on wires. Ice a half-ball of styrofoam and insert wired stems of leaves and berries for a between-the-tiers ornament.

PREPARE TIERS. Bake 16" x 4" square and 12" x 4" round, two-layer tiers. Bake a cake in the Candlelit Tree Pan. Fill and ice the 16" and 12" tiers. Use dowel construction in both tiers as described on page 8. Mark a 6" circle in center of 12" tier, and insert 7 dowels within it. Clip off level with top of tier. Push a 6" round separator plate into top surface of tier to support tree, and conceal with icing. Ice the tree cake thinly and place on stand. Assemble lower tiers on a 20" square cake board. Use 12" separator plates and 5" Grecian pillars.

DECORATE TREE TIER. Make many small bows from gilt ribbon. Pipe "leaves" on tree with tube 74, pulling them out into points. Attach bows to tree with icing and secure a Winged Angel at top.

DECORATE BASE TIER. Pipe tube 8 bottom ball border. Divide each side of tier into fourths. Drop string guidelines, then pipe a tube 125 ruffle from point to point, extending over the bottom border. Using ruffles as guide, drop string guidelines from top edge of tier. Pipe a tube 104 double ribbon swag from point to point. Edge separator plate with tube 7 curves. Pipe tube 7 top ball border. Pipe tube 104 scallops on top of tier over border. Finish with tube 104 bows on tier side.

DECORATE MIDDLE TIER. Pipe a tube 8 ball border around base of tier, then pipe a tube 125 ruffle over it. Divide the center of the side of the tier into twelfths, drop string guidelines and pipe tube 104 ribbon swags. Add tube 7 top border. Pipe tube 104 scallops on top of tier, lining up with swags on side. On the side of the tier, attach three holly leaves at each intersection of the swags with icing. Pipe tube 6 berries.

ADD FINISHING TOUCHES. Secure the holly orna-ment between the pillars with icing. Make four bows from gilt ribbon and wire to base of each pillar. Set the Christmas tree on top of the cake and add a large gilt bow to the base. The bride will freeze the tree cake for the first anniversary. Two lower tiers serve 196 guests.

Mistletoe *Shown on page 67*

Snow white tiers are hung with symbolic mistletoe to create a very romantic bridal cake.

MAKE MISTLETOE FIRST. Attach squares of wax paper on a curved surface. Pipe a dot with tube 2 and push a short length of fine florists' wire into the wet icing. Dry, then pipe an elongated leaf over each dot with tube 7. Do larger leaves with tube 9. Brush the leaves to taper at the wire. Dry, then wrap stems with floral tape. Make clusters by taping leaves together, one in top center, others on either side below it. Then pipe tube 2 white berries. Paint a dot of black food color on each berry. You will need nine clusters.

PREPARE ORNAMENTS. For top ornament, glue the Gate-Top Arch to top plate from Heart Base, then glue two 2½" White Birds in front of it. Wire a mistletoe cluster to top of arch, then add ribbon bows. For ornament below top tier, trim a 4" Filigree Heart with two bows and a cluster of mistletoe. For ornament below middle tier, glue a 4" Filigree Heart to the Petite Heart Base and dry. Trim with mistletoe and ribbon. Pipe tiny tube 1 mistletoe on a Kissing Angel figure.

PREPARE TWO-LAYER TIERS. Bake 16" x 4", 12" x 4" and 8" x 3" round tiers. Fill and ice. Assemble on a 20" ruffle-edged cake board. Raise 12" tier with 14" separator plates and 7½" Corinthian pillars. Elevate the 8" tier with 10" separator plates and 5" Corinthian pillars.

DECORATE BOTTOM TIER. All tier sides are trimmed with fluffy flourishes and curves of icing. Pipe tube 22 base shell border. At center front and back, mark side with a 3" heart cookie cutter. Use tube 16 for all side trim. Outline hearts with curved feathered shells, then pipe six evenly spaced fleurs-de-lis on either side of hearts. Connect fleurs-de-lis with a curve and add shells and stars. Drop strings over base border and finish with stars. Edge separator plate with tube 18 and pipe reverse shell top border with the same tube.

DECORATE MIDDLE TIER. Pipe eight evenly spaced tube 18 upright shells at base of tier. Top each with a star and fill in bottom border with shells, using same tube. Using a 2″ cutter, mark hearts on side of tier between each upright shell. Outline and connect hearts with feathered curves, using tube 16. Edge separator plate and do reverse shell top border with tube 17.

DECORATE TOP TIER. Pipe tube 17 bottom shell border. Pipe eight evenly spaced fleurs-de-lis on side of tier, using tube 16. Connect with strings and add shells and stars with same tube. Pipe reverse shell top border with tube 16.

ADD FINISHING TOUCHES. Attach heart ornaments between pillars. Set the Kissing Angels on base tier. Attach clusters of mistletoe in the two hearts piped on bottom tier. Trim each lower pillar with a cluster of mistletoe and a bow. Set arch ornament on top of cake. Mistletoe is ready to star at the reception! Two lower tiers serve 186, top tier serves an additional 30.

A cheery cake for the groom
A wreath of scarlet poinsettias trims this latticed cake in his favorite flavor.

PIPE FLOWERS FIRST. Make royal icing poinsettias. Begin by piping a circle of eight petals with tube 74, then pipe a circle of eight more petals on top with tube 75. Add tube 1 center dots, first green, then yellow, then tiny red dots on yellow.

DECORATE CAKE. Bake a 9″ x 13″ x 4″ two-layer sheet cake. Fill, then ice sides with Chocolate Buttercream, top with cream-color buttercream (substitute butter for shortening in recipe on page 126). Set on a 13″ x 17″ foil-covered cake board.

Use Beautiful Bridal pattern to mark lattice areas on top and sides. Pipe lattice with tube 2, starting in center of areas and working to either side. Outline curved edges with tube 14 shells.

Pipe tube 18 shells around base of cake, tube 17 shells around top edge and down the corners. Mark a 6″ circle on top of cake and attach poinsettias on dots of icing. Pipe mounds of icing on corners at base of cake and press in poinsettias. Trim all flowers with tube 67 leaves. This groom's cake serves wedding-sized pieces to 54.

Orchids have always been considered the ultimate floral tribute to a beloved lady—so White Orchid is an outstanding finale to our calendar of flower-trimmed bridal cakes.

The corsage of ruffled flowers and ivy leaves is made of gum paste. After the reception is over, it can be set beneath a glass dome to serve as a lovely memento of the glorious wedding day.

The tiny square cake with its orchid trim is for the bride to freeze for the first anniversary.

Decorate the bridal cake

Make orchids and ivy leaves well in advance, then the cake can be decorated quite quickly and easily. The square tiers make serving easy.

CREATE GUM PASTE TRIMS. Make seven gum paste orchids and two sizes of ivy leaves using the Flower Garden Cutter Set. Follow the directions for the making the orchids and ivy in the instruction booklet that accompanies the cutters. Wrap the stems of the completed orchids with floral tape. When the ivy leaves are dry, bind them into clusters of three with floral tape. To make the corsage, tape the stems of five orchids and about six clusters of ivy leaves together into a long, narrow grouping with floral tape and add a fluffy ribbon bow. Secure the corsage to a Petite Heart Base with icing.

Tape six leaves to an orchid for a miniature corsage to trim the first anniversary cake. Add a ribbon bow. Secure the little corsage to a Petite Heart Base. Remove the tulle and artifical flowers from Bridal Bells ornament. Secure clusters of ivy leaves within the bells on mounds of icing. Attach the remaining orchid to the ornament by securing the stem to the lower portion of the heart with floral tape. Add a ribbon bow.

PREPARE THE TIERS. Bake 18″ x 4″ and 12″ x 4″ square, two-layer tiers. Bake two layers in 5″ square pans for the anniversary cake. Fill and ice them smoothly. Set 5″ cake on a 7″ foil-covered cake board. Place the 18″ tier on a 22″ square,

foil-covered cake board. Elevate the 12″ tier with 13″ square separator plates and 7½″ Corinthian pillars. Before placing the pillars in position between the separator plates, wind ¼″ ribbons around each, securing the ends inside the pillars with tape. Wire a bow to the top of each pillar.

DECORATE BASE TIER. Divide each side of tier into eighths. Pipe a tube 20 bottom shell border, then pipe eight tube 126 ribbon swags above the border. Pipe a tube 124 bow in the center of each side of the tier. Edge the separator plate with tube 17 curved shells. Pipe tube 17 top shell border, then add tube 126 ribbon swags on top of the tier, lining up with swags below.

DECORATE UPPER TIER. Divide sides of tier into eighths. Pipe tube 20 bottom shell border, then pipe eight tube 124 ribbon swags above the border. Pipe a tube 124 bow on each corner of the tier. Mark an 8½″ circle in the center of the top of the tier with a toothpick. Outline the circle with tube 124 ribbon swags. Add a tube 17 top shell border.

DECORATE THE ANNIVERSARY CAKE. Pipe tube 17 shells around the base of the cake, then pipe four tube 104 ribbon swags just above the shells. At each corner, pipe a tube 102 bow, then add a tube 17 top shell border.

ADD THE FINISHING TOUCHES. Mix equal parts of granulated sugar and edible glitter. Brush 24 Lacy Bells, 1¼″ x 1⅛″, with egg white and as each is brushed, sprinkle it with the sugar and glitter mixture. Let dry, then attach three bells in the center of each piped bow on the base tier with small mounds of icing. Attach two bells in the centers of the piped bows on the upper tier. Secure the ornament to the top of the cake and the corsage between the pillars.

Attach a bell to each corner of the anniversary cake, then set miniature corsage on top.

White Orchid will serve 234 wedding guests.

CHAPTER FOUR

Distinctive bridal cakes that explore the horizons of the decorator's art

The cakes in this chapter were designed for the decorator's delight—and of course for the pleasure of the bride. These masterpieces display the possibilities of decorating techniques—lavish borders, curving line work, the most fragile lace, hanging loops and lattice. See the magic that can be achieved with gum paste—oval medallions to accent tiers, a quaint little village church, a unique wedding ornament with a trio of cherubs on a baroque base. Figure piping creates lovebirds and colorful clusters of fruit. When flowers are used on these cakes, they complement the other trim.

All the cakes will serve from 110 to more than 200 guests. Many are accompanied by harmonizing groom's cakes or shower cakes.

First love

Lovely to look at and very quick to decorate! Lavish-looking borders are the feature of this cake, and arrangements of fresh flowers set them off. A ring cake frames the flowers at the top.

PREPARE ORNAMENT to place between the pillars. Paint the flat side of the 6″ plate from Crystal Clear Cake Divider set with thinned green royal icing. Dry, then paint again and dry. Attach the Old-Fashioned Fence around the edge of the plate with icing and set the Bridal Couple within it.

BAKE THE TWO-LAYER TIERS, 16″ x 4″ square and 12″ x 4″ square. Bake the top tier in the Ring-Shaped Mold. Fill the two square tiers and ice, then ice the ring tier. Secure the 16″ tier to a 20″ ruffle-edged cake board. Mark position of pillars on 16″ tier by lightly pressing with a 13″ square separator plate. Place a 7½″ Corinthian pillar at each mark. Push a ¼″ diameter dowel rod through each pillar and the tier, down to the cake board. Mark tops of pillars on the dowels, lift up and clip off ⅞″ below the marks. Push dowels back down to the board.

Secure the 12″ tier to a 13″ square separator plate.

Lightly mark a 10″ circle on top and insert seven dowel rods, clipped level with top, within it. Set ring tier on 12″ round separator plate, then push into 12″ tier. Place tiers on pillars.

DECORATE BASE TIER. Divide each side of tier in thirds, beginning 2″ in from each corner. In center of space within marks, pipe a tube 19 elongated shell, then pipe two more on either side of it. Below the shells pipe two comma-shaped curves with the same tube. Pipe a ruffled fan between the curves with tube 104. Fill the ruffle center with a tube 19 rosette. Pipe the same design at each mark, and one on each corner.

Push plate on prepared ornament into top of tier, between the pillars, and edge it with tube 17 rosettes. Add reverse shell top border with the same tube. Glue three 1¼″ glittered bells and a bow to one pillar.

DECORATE MIDDLE TIER. On each corner, pipe the same design as on the base tier, then complete base border with tube 19 rosettes. Pipe the same design in upside down position in center of tier sides. Add a tube 19 top shell border.

ON THE RING TIER, pipe tube 19 base shell border and tube 18 top shell border.

ADD FRESH FLOWERS. Fill a Heart Bowl with Oasis, add water and set White Bird in center. Arrange flowers in bowl. Use the same flowers the bride carries in her bouquet. You may arrange the flowers in advance and refrigerate them until ready to be placed on the cake. Secure the bowl in the center of the ring tier with icing.

At the reception, insert one Flower Spike into the top of the 12″ tier at the right front corner, and two spikes into the 16″ tier at the left front corner. Fill spikes with a little water using an eye dropper and arrange flowers in them. The two lower tiers of First Love serve 200, top tier an additional 34.

It's pretty, it's feminine, it's covered with rich chocolate fondant! Fine line piping circles the tiers. Everyone will love its sweet continental air, and enjoy its delicious flavor. For true chocolate lovers, bake the tiers from a chocolate cake recipe and fill the layers with Chocolate Canache or Chocolate Buttercream.

How to decorate Pirouette

IN ADVANCE, make marzipan roses as described on page 102. Paint four 5″ Grecian pillars and a 9″ round separator plate with thinned royal icing in a delicate pink. Dry.

MAKE TOP ORNAMENT. Tape Beautiful Bridal pattern to stiff board and tape wax paper over it. Do lattice with tube 2 and royal icing, add scroll edge with tube 13. Dry, turn over and pipe scroll edge again. Cut a 4″ circle from chocolate-tinted marzipan, or make a circle using Color Flow technique. When dry, attach the lattice pieces to it, as described on page 102.

BAKE THE TWO-LAYER TIERS. Bake 16″ x 4″, 12″ x 4″ and 8″ x 4″ round tiers. Fill and ice with Chocolate Buttercream, then cover with Chocolate Poured Fondant. (See recipe on page 128.) You will need three recipes for the base tier, two for the middle tier and one for the top tier. To cover the large base tier, start pouring the fondant about 3″ from the top edge. When side is covered, fill remaining area of top. Let fondant set.

Assemble tiers on a 20″ foil-covered, ruffle-edged board using dowels in base tier for support (see page 8). Lightly mark the position of the pillars on the 12″ tier with a 9″ separator plate. Set pillars in position on tier, and insert a dowel rod down to plastic-wrapped cake circle below tier. Mark tops of pillars on dowels, lift up and clip off ⅞″ below marks. Push dowels down again.

DECORATE BASE TIER. Pipe tube 8 triple ball border around base. Divide side of tier into twenty-fourths. All line trim on tier is done with tube 3. Drop strings from point to point, about halfway down on side of tier. Drop another set of strings below them. Now pipe curves, tear drops and dots as picture shows. Using side trim as guide, pipe scallops on top of tier and top with dots.

ON MIDDLE TIER, pipe tube 6 triple ball border around base of tier. Divide side of tier into sixteenths and pipe tube 3 curves, dots and fleurs-de-lis within the divisions. Pipe tube 3 scallops and dots on top. Set marzipan roses between pillars on small dots of icing.

ON TOP TIER, pipe tube 6 ball border around base. Divide side of tier into twelfths. Within divisions, drop double strings, and add dots and fleurs-de-lis with tube 3. Pipe tube 3 scallops and dots on tier top. Set ornament on top of tier and attach roses with icing. Two lower tiers of Pirouette serve 186 guests, top tier serves 30.

A companion cake for the groom

Pipe roses in Chocolate Canache or buttercream and refrigerate until cake is ready to be served.

Bake and fill a two-layer cake, 12″ round. Ice smoothly with white buttercream, then cover with pink-tinted poured fondant (page 127). Let fondant harden. Set cake on a 16″ tray or cake board. Transfer pattern to top of cake. Pipe lattice with tube 2 and edge with tube 3 beading.

Divide side of cake into sixteenths and pipe a free hand scroll within each division with tube 3. Pipe tube 4 stems and attach roses with dots of icing. Add tube 66 leaves. The cake cuts into 68 wedding cake-size servings.

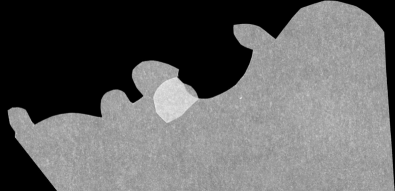

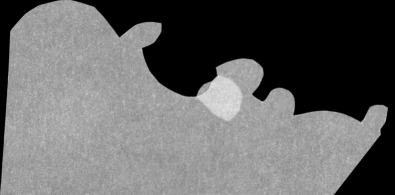

Exquisite lace pieces, piped on Australian nails, circle this bridal cake, and create a delicate crown on the top tier. Subtle color contributes to the charm of Antique Lace. The cake is covered with cream-colored buttercream (use butter instead of shortening in recipe on page 126), and the lace is piped in ecru royal icing.

Make trims in advance

MAKE LACE PIECES using Australian net nails, egg white royal icing, tube 2 and Beautiful Bridal patterns. Transfer patterns to parchment paper and cut out. To secure patterns to nails, rub nail with solid white shortening and smooth pattern onto it. Rub again with shortening, apply a piece of wax paper—cut same as pattern—and rub with shortening. Make ten pieces piped on inner side of Crescent nail for middle tier and ten oval pieces on Arch nail for top tier. Pipe ten pieces on both sides of the Large Border nail for base tier. For these pieces, simply grease nail, then pipe pattern free-hand directly on it, using pattern as guide.

After piping, push nails in styrofoam to dry, then place in warm oven a few minutes. Carefully remove lace pieces. Make extras as the lace is fragile.

FOR ORNAMENTS, pipe two left and two right half-hearts and two full hearts on a flat surface. Dry, then assemble. Attach wire to center of each full heart with icing and dry. Insert exposed wire into styrofoam so point of heart rests on the styrofoam. Attach a right and a left half-heart to each full heart at 90° angles with lines of royal icing. Prop until dry with cotton balls.

PIPE FLOWERS. Make many royal icing drop flowers with tubes 26 and 35. Pipe tube 2 centers. Dry.

PAINT PLASTIC PIECES with thinned royal icing—a 14″ round separator plate, four 5″ Corinthian pillars and four Musical Trio cherubs. Dry.

Decorate the cake

BAKE, FILL AND ICE 16″ x 4″, 12″ x 4″ and 6″ x 3″ round two-layer tiers. Place base tier on a 20″ cake board. Mark position of pillars on top of base tier by pressing lightly with a 14″ round separator plate. Place a 5″ Corinthian pillar at each mark, then push a long dowel rod down through each pillar and tier to cake board. Mark tops of pillars on dowels, lift and clip off ⅞″ below marks. Push dowels back down to board. Secure middle tier to 14″ separator plate and position top tier on it.

DECORATE BASE TIER. Pipe tube 8 triple base ball border. Push wire on assembled heart into top of tier, then attach drop flowers around it and pillars.

Divide top edge of tier into tenths and mark. Drop tube 2 triple strings within marks, keeping strings 1″ from each mark. Pipe a curve of dots below strings. At each division, secure a Large Border lace piece, attaching to top of tier with lines of icing. Hold until icing sets. Pipe tube 1 dots on edges of lace. Attach flowers below lace pieces. Pipe tube 7 top ball border.

DECORATE UPPER TIERS. Pipe a tube 7 triple ball border around base of middle tier. Divide the top edge into tenths and drop triple tube 2 strings and dots. Pipe tube 5 top ball border.

On top tier, pipe a tube 6 base ball border. Using strings on middle tier as guide, drop ten guidelines on lower side of tier. Attach garlands of flowers. Push wire on heart ornament into top of tier. Secure painted cherubs. Pipe tube 5 ball border around top edge, then secure oval lace pieces over edge of tier with dots of icing, lining up with flower garlands. Pipe tube 1 dots on edges of lace.

Secure lace crescents to top of middle tier with icing, lining them up with the strings on tier side. Trim edges of lace with tube 1 dots. Secure flowers within the curve of each crescent. Trim all flowers with tube 65 leaves. On edge of separator plate, drop tube 2 overlapping strings. (Note: this must be done after the cake is reassembled on the reception table.) Two lower tiers serve 186, top tier 16.

Curves of see-through lattice give feminine charm to this imposing cake. Dainty forget-me-nots add the traditional "something blue".

Decorate the bridal cake

MAKE TRIMS IN ADVANCE. Pipe many forget-me-nots with tubes 101 and 102. Add tube 2 centers.

Pipe off-the-cake lattice with tube 2 and egg white royal icing. Tape Beautiful Bridal heart pattern to a 6″ curved surface and tape wax paper over. Pipe lattice and outline, dry, then pipe tube 2 beading around edge. Use the back of the Egg Minicake pan to pipe six dimensional oval pieces. Lightly grease back of cups with solid white vegetable shortening. Pipe a line around the cups about ½″ up from base. Pipe lattice, then over-pipe outline and dry. To remove from pan, place in warm oven a few moments and carefully lift off ovals.

Glue Bridal Couple to Heart Base. Secure forget-me-nots to base with dots of icing. Trim Wedding Chime ornament with flowers.

BAKE, FILL AND ICE 18″ x 4″, 12″ x 4″ and 8″ x 4″ round two-layer tiers. Assemble on a 24″ cake board using 14″ round separator plates, 10¼″ Roman pillars and dowel construction (page 8).

DECORATE BASE TIER. Divide top edge into twelfths. Mark scallops within divisions with a 3″ round cutter on top and side of tier. Pipe tube 8 bottom ball border. Drop guidelines for large and small garlands at base of tier, using top scallops as a guide. Pipe garlands with tube 8 zigzags and over-pipe with tube 7. Add tube 2 strings and dots. Edge separator plate with tube 8 balls. Following marked scallops, pipe upper garlands with tube 8 zigzags, then over-pipe twice with tube 6. Fill in spaces between garlands and edge of cake with tube 2 lattice. Edge with tube 4. Secure flowers.

ON MIDDLE TIER, pipe tube 8 bottom ball border. Divide side of tier into twelfths. Pipe tube 8 zigzag garlands from point to point, then over-pipe with tube 7. Add two tube 2 strings and dots. Secure lattice ovals to side of tier in center of every other garland with lines of icing. Edge with tube 2 beading and trim with forget-me-nots. Pipe tube 7 reverse bulb top border.

ON TOP TIER, pipe tube 8 bottom ball border and tube 6 top ball border. Attach lattice hearts with icing to side of tier. Trim tier with forget-me-nots. Secure ornament to top with icing.

ADD FINISHING TOUCHES. Secure ornament between pillars. Add a sprinkling of flowers. Make four groups of bells by gluing three 1″ filigree bells together. Glue bells to pillars near top and add bows. Top tier serves 30, two lower tiers 216.

Make the dainty shower cake

MAKE HEART ORNAMENT. Tape heart pattern to flat surface and cover with wax paper. Pipe lattice and outline with tube 2 and egg white royal icing. Twist two pieces of florists' wire into a "Y" (see pattern). Turn dried heart over and attach wire to back along outline with royal icing. Dry, then turn over and pipe tube 3 beading around edge. Make a hole in the top plate of the Petite Heart Base with a heated nail. Ornament will be assembled on cake.

BAKE A TWO-LAYER CAKE, 10″ x 4″ round. Fill, ice, and place on serving tray. Pipe tube 8 bottom ball border. Divide side of cake into twelfths and pipe a tube 8 zigzag garland at base from point to point. Over-pipe with tube 7 and top with tube 3 strings. On top edge of cake, drop triple tube 3 strings using lower garlands as guide. Add tube 7 top ball border and pipe message on cake top with tube 2. Center heart plate on cake top and insert wire on lattice heart through hole and down into cake. Trim cake with tube 101 forget-me-nots and tube 65 leaves. Serves dessert-sized portions to 14.

Two pink satin bows tie up a snow-white cake for a pretty young bride. Heavily piped fleurs-de-lis give light and shadow to the tiers. Wedding Present is very quick to decorate. A nosegay of piped roses is placed between the pillars, but you can personalize the cake by using fresh flowers that duplicate the bride's bouquet.

How to decorate Wedding Present

PIPE ABOUT TWO DOZEN ROSES with tube 104 and royal icing. Dry, then mount all but three on wire stems. Pipe tube 65 leaves on wires. (See page 14.) Twist stems together to form a bouquet, adding a ruffle of tulle. Tie with a ribbon bow.

BAKE, FILL AND ICE 18″ x 4″ round, 10″ x 4″ square and 6″ x 3″ round, two-layer tiers. Assemble on 22″ cake board. Use 11″ square separator plates and 7½″ Corinthian pillars.

DIVIDE SIDE OF BOTTOM TIER into sixteenths, marking 1½″ from cake board. (Use pillars as guide.) Pipe two tube 32 curving shells from base of tier to each marked point. Complete bottom border with tube 32 stars. Top each pair of shells with a tube 18 fleur-de-lis and star. Edge lower separator plate with tube 16. Mark scallops around top of tier with a 1¾″ cutter. Pipe the scallops with tube 13, then pipe tube 20 top star border.

ON SIDE OF MIDDLE TIER, repeat the elements of the side border on base tier. Pipe curving shells with tube 22, fill in stars with same tube and do fleurs-de-lis and finishing stars with tube 17. With same tube, pipe a fleur-de-lis on top of tier at each corner, and do top star border.

ON TOP TIER, pipe tube 18 base star border and tube 17 top star border. Divide side into eighths and pipe a tube 17 fleur-de-lis at each point.

ADD FINISHING TOUCHES. Glue Petite Bridal Couple and 7″ Filigree Heart to Petite Heart Base. Wire a fluffy bow to ornament and one pillar. Secure ornament to cake top and add a few flowers beside it. Place bouquet between pillars. Two lower tiers serve 198, top tier serves 16.

Surprise . . . for a shower party

Preview the bridal cake with this charming shower or engagement cake.

PREPARE ORNAMENT. Glue Stand-Up Kissing Couple and 7″ Filigree Heart to Heart Base. Wire two bows to ornament. Pipe roses and buds with tubes 103 and 104 and mount on wires. Pipe leaves on wires with tube 65. Tape into a spray.

DECORATE CAKE. Bake, fill and ice a 9″ x 13″ two-layer sheet cake. Place on cake board. Divide long sides into sixths and short sides into fourths. Pipe the bottom border the same as base tier of Wedding Present, making shells and stars with tube 32 and fleurs-de-lis with tube 17. Mark scallops on cake top with a 1¾″ cookie cutter. Pipe tube 2 message. Pipe tube 14 top star border, then pipe scallops with same tube. Secure ornament to cake and add spray. Serves 24 dessert-size slices.

Build the gum paste church

CUT OUT PIECES following Beautiful Bridal patterns. Make a recipe of gum paste (page 128). Tint about half violet for walls, a fourth blue for roofs and door. Leave a small amount of the remaining fourth untinted for windows, and tint the rest pink for walkway. Reserve the pink gum paste. *All pieces are rolled about 1/16" thick on cornstarch-dusted surface, cut with a sharp X-acto knife, and dried flat about 24 hours.* Cut roof pieces first and immediately press in marks for the shingles with tube 100. Cut remaining pieces. Check dried pieces with patterns for accuracy. If needed, carefully trim with knife. Hand-model a ½" bell and insert a knotted thread through top. Cut styrofoam supports and ice thinly with royal icing.

TRANSFER WINDOW MARKINGS to the gum paste pieces and pipe royal icing lines with tube 1. Dry, then fill areas with tinted piping gel. Pipe royal icing trim on door and pipe tube 1 cornices and cross on wax paper.

ASSEMBLE CHURCH, using royal icing for glue. *Dry after each step.* Attach windows to church sides and tower front, then attach door brace to lower front. Attach two side walls of main church to styrofoam support. Pipe lines of icing on vertical edges and attach front and back walls. Add the two roof sections, holding in place till icing sets. Secure tower support to front of church, add side walls, then front and back walls. Add tower roof.

Assemble steeple walls. Lay a piece of florists' wire across top of walls, clip to length and secure with icing. Hang bell from wire. Attach steeple roof sections to walls. Glue steeple to tower roof. Pipe icing lines on top edges of door brace, attach door roof sections and hold in place till icing sets. Pipe icing lines on vertical edges of door frame and attach doors. Finally, pipe a ball of icing on point of steeple roof and set in cross. Spray with two coats of clear acrylic glaze to protect from moisture. Attach church to cardboard base.

Decorate the cake

MAKE ROYAL ICING TRIMS. Pipe many drop flowers using tubes 129, 191 and 225. Add tube 2 centers. Figure pipe 46 bells. Pipe a ball of icing with tube 6, then circle with tube 4 for bell edge and add a dot.

PREPARE THE TIERS. Paint the top of a 14" round separator plate with thinned green royal icing and dry. Bake, fill and ice 16" x 4", 12" x 4" and 8" x 3" square, two-layer tiers. *Use boiled icing to cover this cake.* Spread green icing on the top of the 8" tier and pat with a damp sponge for a grassy effect. Assemble the tiers on a 20" square cake board. Center painted separator plate on top of base tier

and raise the top tiers with a 13" square separator plate and 7½" Corinthian pillars.

DECORATE BASE TIER. Pipe tube 20 bottom shell border. Divide each side of the tier into thirds, starting 2" in from each corner. Drop string guidelines and pipe tube 17 zigzag garlands between the divisions. Attach flowers to garlands with dots of icing. Above garlands, pipe tube 3 bows, then attach bells. Edge separator plate with tube 16, then pipe top shell border with the same tube. Secure flowers around the base of each pillar and to Petite Dainty Charm ornament. Secure ornament between the pillars.

DECORATE UPPER TIERS. Roll reserved pink gum paste as thin as possible, then cut a 1½" x 12" strip for the walkway. Dampen walkway area on tiers, then attach gum paste strip as pictured. Edge with tube 3 beading. Pipe a tube 20 bottom shell border, tube 16 top border on middle tier. Pipe two tube 17 zigzag garlands on each side of tier extending them to the top edge of the tier on the front. Attach drop flowers with dots of icing. Pipe tube 3 bows and attach piped bells.

On top tier, pipe tube 19 upright shells around base and add tube 16 stars. Set church on cake and attach drop flowers around it and along walkway. Pipe upright tube 17 stars for top border. Trim all flowers with tube 65 leaves. Two lower tiers of Wedding Bells serve 200, top tier 32.

Floating, suspended loops of icing adorn this cake that will impress everyone at the reception. This technique requires a light, rhythmic touch, but with practice, is not hard to do. Iridescent trims and white violets add to the fragile effect.

MAKE ROYAL ICING FLOWERS IN ADVANCE. Pipe about 275 violets with tube 101, add tube 1 dots in the centers and dry. Mount about 50 violets on wire stems (see page 14). Pipe tube 65 leaves on wires and dry. Tape most of the stemmed violets and leaves into a bouquet for the top of the cake.

CREATE TOP ORNAMENT. Clip top loops off of 3″ and 1½″ Iridescent Bells. Glue tops of bells together, smaller at base. Glue four more 1½″ bells around base bell. Put bouquet in vase.

BAKE, FILL AND ICE 15″ x 4″, 12″ x 4″ and 9″ x 3″ two-layer petal tiers. Cut a petal-shaped cake board 19″ at widest point. Cover with foil, edge with ruffle and set 15″ tier on it. Fold a 13″ paper circle in eighths and cut scallop pattern for top of base tier. Transfer to tier with toothpick. Center a 12″ round separator plate on the tier to mark position of pillars. Set Iridescent pillars on marks and insert dowel rods through pillars down to cake board. Mark tops of pillars on dowels, lift up and clip off ⅞″ below marks. Push dowels down to cake board again. Place 12″ tier on a 12″ round separator plate and center 9″ tier on top of it.

DECORATE BASE TIER. Pipe tube 8 bottom ball border. *Use egg white royal icing for all string work.* Drop seven tube 1 loops from top edge of each petal of tier, making center loop larger than the others. Attach more loops to these to form design, as picture shows. Add dot trim. Pipe tube 7 top ball border and outline scallop pattern with tube 5. Drop string guidelines and attach garlands of violets on each petal. Pipe tube 65 leaves.

Pipe a crescent of icing with a large tube on top of tier. Attach Iridescent Grapes, stemmed violets and leaves and unstemmed violets to the crescent. Add a few tube 65 leaves and secure Petite Bridal Couple in front.

ON 12″ TIER, pipe tube 7 bottom ball border. On each petal, drop tube 1 strings, using same technique as on base tier. Add dot trim. Pipe tube 6 top ball border. Attach clusters of violets at base of tier and pipe tube 65 leaves.

ON 9″ TIER, pipe tube 6 bottom ball border. Drop tube 1 strings using same technique as on base tier. Add dot trim. Pipe tube 6 top ball border. Secure two violets between each petal and pipe tube 65 leaves. Secure the ornament to the top of the cake with icing.

PIPE SUSPENDED LOOPS. This must be done after the cake is assembled at the reception. *Use boiled or egg white royal icing and let each row of loops dry before piping the next.* Begin by dropping tube 1 loops from each scallop of separator plate. At each pillar drop rows of loops, attaching each to a loop above. Use the picture as a guide. Do not let the suspended loops touch the bottom tier. Two lower tiers of Bridal Veil serve 106, top tier serves 20.

BAKE, FILL AND ICE two-layer hexagon tiers—15″ x 4″, 12″ x 4″ and 9″ x 3″. Set tiers on corresponding cake boards and edge base tier with ruffle. Place 14″ board, stud plates down, on 15″ tier to mark the position of the pillars, then remove. Mark the top of the 12″ tier with the 11″ board. Set 5″ Corinthian pillars in marked positions on two lower tiers. Push dowel rods through pillars, down to cake boards. Mark tops of pillars on dowels, lift up and clip off at marks. Push dowels down again.

DECORATE THE BASE TIER. Pipe tube 8 bottom ball border. On each side of the hexagon, drop a tube 4 guideline for the garlands. Attach flowers with dots of icing. Pipe freehand scroll pattern above garland with tube 4 and over-pipe with tube 2. Pipe scrolls in lower corners with tube 5, over-pipe with tube 3. Add top ball border with tube 6. Pipe tube 2 loops of blue icing at corners. Center the large gum paste hexagon on the tier top and edge with tube 2 beading.

DECORATE THE MIDDLE TIER. Pipe tube 6 bottom ball border. Attach a large gum paste oval to each side with icing. Edge each plaque with tube 2 beading, then pipe tube 3 freehand scrolls around it. Over-pipe the scrolls with tube 1. Pipe graduated dots with tube 3 above and below ovals. Add a fleur-de-lis at each bottom corner with tube 5, then pipe top ball border with the same tube. Center the medium gum paste hexagon on the tier top and edge with tube 2 beading.

DECORATE THE TOP TIER. Pipe tube 5 bottom ball border. On the two small gum paste ovals pipe the initials of the happy couple with tube 2, over-pipe with tube 1. Dry, then attach the plaques to the back and front of the tier with icing. Edge ovals with tube 2 beading, then add tube 3 scroll-work around them. Over-pipe the scrolls with tube 1. Pipe graduated tube 3 dots above and below ovals. Pipe scrolls on remaining sides of tier, near top, with tube 3, over-pipe with tube 1. Below scrolls, and covering two sides of tier, drop tube 4 guidelines for garlands. Attach wild roses with dots of icing. Pipe tube 4 top ball border. Center small gum paste hexagon on top of tier, then edge with tube 2 beading.

ADD FINISHING TOUCHES. Attach Musical Trio cherubs to top of base tier. Trim with flowers. Attach the Angel Fountain to middle tier. Trim with flowers. Secure ornament to the top of the cake and add flowers. Trim all flowers with tube 65 leaves. The top tier of Blue Medallion serves 22, two lower tiers 116 guests.

Curving scrolls piped and over-piped, give a lavish sculptural look to the tiers, dimensional gum paste ovals add color accent, flower garlands repeat the curves. Blue Medallion is a unique cake for a formal bridal reception.

MAKE ROYAL ICING WILD ROSES in advance using tubes 102, 103 and 104. Add tube 1 stamens. Dry all within a curved surface.

MAKE MEDALLIONS. Make a recipe of gum paste (page 128) and tint a portion of it blue. Roll out about 1/16″ thick on cornstarch-dusted surface. Using Beautiful Bridal patterns, cut three hexagon plates and dry flat. Cut two small ovals and dry on cornstarch-dusted 5″ plastic egg mold. Cut six larger ovals and dry on the Egg Pan, dusted with cornstarch to prevent sticking.

PREPARE CAKE BOARDS for each tier. Using pans as guide, cut an 11″ and a 14″ hexagon from double thickness corrugated cardboard. Cut a 19″ hexagon from four thicknesses of cardboard. Cover smoothly with foil. On the bottom of each of the two smaller boards, about 1″ in from the corners, glue six stud plates.

A special charm is given to this happy cake by icing the tiers in three harmonizing pastels. Snowy borders are quickly done and set off the dainty tints.

MAKE MANY DROP FLOWERS in royal icing with tubes 35, 129 and 225. Add tube 2 centers and dry. Mount about one-third of the flowers on wire stems (page 14). Pipe tube 66 leaves on wires. When dry, arrange stemmed flowers and leaves into two bouquets and tie each with a ribbon bow.

BAKE, FILL AND ICE two-layer heart tiers—15" x 4", 12" x 4" and 9" x 3". Assemble on a 19" ruffle-edged board, cut in heart shape. Use dowel construction as described on page 8.

DECORATE BASE TIER. Pipe tube 4B upright shells around bottom of tier. Pipe tube 3 overlapping double strings from the tops of the shells. Top each shell with a tube 18 star and add a top shell border with the same tube.

ON MIDDLE TIER, pipe tube 18 rosettes around bottom. Divide each side of heart into eighths, then pipe tube 3 triple strings from point to point. Top intersections with tube 16 stars and add top shell border with the same tube.

ON TOP TIER, pipe tube 16 rosette border around base of tier. Divide each side of heart into eighths and pipe tube 3 double strings from point to point. Add stars and do top shell border with tube 16. Secure Holly Hobbie's Wishing Well* in center of tier and trim with flowers. With a large tube, pipe a line around ornament base. Cover with flowers, attaching with dots of icing. Add tube 65 leaves.

The little bouquets are for the mothers of the bride and groom. The two lower tiers of Heart's Delight serve 138, the top tier serves an additional 28 guests.

Happy-go-lucky, a shower cake

This darling shower cake topped by a quaint antique car is sure to bring smiles from the guests. Decorate it very quickly and easily.

PIPE ROYAL ICING DROP FLOWERS with tubes 35, 129 and 225 in advance. Add tube 2 centers and dry. Cut a thin 2" x 1¼" card from gum paste (recipe, page 128) and dry flat. Or cut a card from colored paper. Pipe tube 1s lettering on card.

BAKE, FILL AND ICE a 9" x 13" two-layer sheet cake. Bake a cake in the Car Minicake pan. Set sheet cake on a 13" x 17" cake board. Cut a cardboard cake base the same size and shape as the car cake, wrap in clear plastic and secure cake to it. Ice thinly. Place car cake on sheet cake.

DECORATE CAKE. Outline the areas of car cake with tube 3. Pipe steering wheel and wheel spokes with tube 4. Fill in the areas with tube 14 stars and add tube 4 hub caps. Cover the sides of the sheet cake with tube 17 stars. Pipe a tube 4 string from rear of car and trim with tube 101 bows. Trim car with flowers. Mound icing on lower corners of sheet cake and press in flowers. Add tube 66 leaves. Happy-go-lucky serves 24 guests—the car cake is a gift to the groom.

*© American Greetings Corporation

This formal poetic cake is very simply achieved. Patterned swirls of icing enrich the tiers, fresh-looking green ferns give color accent, and the cherub separator set adds distinction.

PIPE FERNS as described on page 14, using tube 65s for the ruffled leaves. Prepare the garden urns by setting a 2″ Filigree Bell on a tube 32 star piped in royal icing on the plate of a Petite Heart Base. Make two urns, and prop until dry. Line with clear plastic, fill with royal icing and insert ferns.

BAKE, FILL AND ICE the two-layer tiers—16″ x 4″ and 12″ x 4″ square, 8″ x 3″ round. Assemble on a ruffle-edged 20″ cake board. Use dowel construction (page 8) and Cupid Pillar Separator set.

DECORATE BASE TIER. Pipe a colonial scroll on tier sides with tube 16, adding swirls and stars with the same tube. Pipe a tube 22 comma-shaped bottom border and a tube 18 top shell border.

DECORATE MIDDLE TIER. Pipe tube 18 bottom shell border. Do all side trim with tube 16. Pipe two large "S"-shaped scrolls on each side of the tier near base. Add two smaller scrolls near top corner of each side, then pipe swirls and extensions. Fill in between large "S" scrolls with "C"-shaped swirls. Pipe tube 16 reverse shell top border. Edge separator plate with tube 13.

DECORATE TOP TIER. Pipe tube 17 bottom shell border. Use tube 16 for side trim. Using pillars as guide, pipe four feathered "C" shapes near base of tier. Connect these swirls with more "C" shapes, rising to top edge of tier. Add curved flourishes, then pipe a reverse shell tube 16 top border. Set a fern-filled urn on separator plate and on top tier, securing with icing. Top tier of Renaissance Garden serves 30, two lower tiers serve 200 guests.

A festive cake for the groom

Clusters of ripe grapes are the dramatic and delicious trim of this chocolate cake.

Bake, fill and ice a two-layer 15″ hexagon cake. Set on a 19″ hexagon-shaped cake board. Pipe tube 21 base border, tube 17 top border. Use tube 17 for remaining trim. On each side of cake, pipe two facing "S" shapes. Add flourishes and connect with a "C" shape near top border. Pipe six similar trims on top of cake.

Fill a little brass cricket box, or other pretty container, with grapes and set on top of cake. Set a cluster of grapes on cake board against each side of cake. Prop with toothpicks if necessary. Garnish with fresh ivy leaves. Serve wedding cake-sized slices to 66 guests.

Two figure piped bluebirds rest on this elegant cake and are its only color accent.

Prepare trims in advance

PIPE THE ROYAL ICING LATTICE HEART. Tape the pattern to a stiff surface and tape wax paper over. Pipe outline of heart and the curving line through the center with tube 4. Pipe the lattice with tube 1 and the leaves with tube 65. Dry thoroughly, then remove the lattice heart from the wax paper. Secure a "Y" of heavy florists' wire to the back of the heart with royal icing and let dry thoroughly. (Use pattern as a guide.)

GLUE PETITE BRIDAL COUPLE to the top plate from the Petite Heart Base.

FIGURE PIPE THE BLUEBIRDS. You will need one facing left and one facing right. Tape the patterns to a stiff, flat surface and tape wax paper over. Do the wings separately. Pipe tube 1 lines of royal icing from the top edge to tip, then brush the lines together with a damp artist's brush and let dry. Pipe the tail of the bird with tube 1 lines, starting at the body. Figure pipe the breast with tube 4, joining it smoothly with the tail. Pipe a ball for the head and continue on to form the back. Slip the dried rear wing under the back and insert the front wing into the body. Pipe the beak with tube 1 and indent icing of the head for the eye. When the bird is dry, brush the breast with thinned pink icing.

Decorate the cake

BAKE, FILL AND ICE the two-layer tiers—14″ x 4″, 10″ x 4″ and 6″ x 3″ round. Assemble on 18″ ruffle-edged cake board using dowel construction (page 8), 8″ round separator plates and 7½″ Corinthian pillars. Set 10″ tier to rear of 14″ tier. Make a hole in the center of an 8″ plate with a heated nail end. Set plate on 10″ tier. Insert wire of lattice heart through plate and tier and steady with icing. Complete assembly of cake.

ON THE 14″ TIER, pipe tube 17 bottom shell border. Divide the side of the tier into eighteenths and drop string guidelines for garlands, center front guideline taking two spaces, next guideline one. Continue for six large curves alternating with six small curves. Pipe tube 17 zigzag garlands over guidelines. Trim with tube 3 strings and tube 66 leaves. Pipe a tube 4 curving vine on side of tier and add tube 66 leaves.

On top of tier pipe twelve evenly-spaced zigzag garlands with tube 16. Add tube 66 leaves. Pipe tube 13 top shell border.

ON THE 10″ TIER, pipe bottom shell border with tube 16. Divide the side of the tier into twelfths and drop string guidelines. Pipe tube 16 zigzag garlands. Trim with tube 3 string and tube 65 leaves. Pipe tube 4 stems on side of tier at center front and back and add tube 65 leaves. Edge the lower separator plate with tube 66 leaves, then surround it with six curves of leaves. Pipe tube 4 vines on pillars and add tube 65 leaves. Pipe tube 13 top shell border.

ON THE 6″ TIER, pipe a tube 15 bottom shell border. Divide the side of the tier into sixths. Drop string guidelines and pipe tube 16 zigzag garlands. Trim with tube 3 strings and tube 65 leaves. Pipe tube 4 stems above garlands and add tube 65 leaves. The top border is tube 65 leaves.

ADD THE FINISHING TOUCHES. Set bride and groom on top of cake. Pipe a nest of tube 66 leaves on center front of bottom tier, and set bluebirds on it. Top tier of Love Song serves 16, two lower tiers serve 140 guests.

There are many times when a decorator needs to decorate a cake in a hurry for an important occasion—and Heaven-sent is a lesson in how to do it beautifully. Fast-to-pipe drop flowers and daintily painted plastic filigree are the secrets.

How to decorate Heaven-sent

PIPE ROYAL ICING DROP FLOWERS with tubes 35, 190 and 225. Pipe tube 2 centers and dry. Paint these plastic pieces with thinned pink royal icing: ten Filigree Swirls, four Filigree Contours, four Snap-On Filigree pillar trims, four 5″ Grecian pillars and five 2″ Lacy Bells.

CREATE ORNAMENTS. Glue two painted filigree Swirls to the top of the plate from the Heart Base near the back and glue a small plastic dove to the top of each. Glue Bridal Couple near the front of the plate. For ornament between pillars, glue one painted bell to the top of the plate from the Petite Heart Base. Glue the four other bells to it, then add a fluffy ribbon bow.

BAKE, FILL AND ICE two-layer tiers—16″ x 4″ round, 10″ x 4″ square and 6″ x 3″ square. Assemble on an 18″ ruffle-edged cake board using 11″ square separator plates, the painted pillars and filigree pillar trims. Use dowel construction (page 8).

ON THE BOTTOM TIER, pipe base rosette border with tube 22. Drop string guidelines, using pillars to measure. Attach flowers on dots of icing. Pipe top shell border with tube 19. Attach filigree swirls to the side of the tier with icing, at 90° angles between the garlands. Secure a cluster of flowers within filigree. Edge separator plate with tube 19. Secure bell ornament between pillars with icing. Add flowers in each bell with dots of icing. Trim pillar bases with flowers. Pipe tube 65 leaves. Attach small plastic doves at ends of garlands.

ON MIDDLE TIER, pipe tube 19 bottom shell border and a tube 17 top shell border. Attach a pair of drop flowers in the center of each side of cake and add tube 65 leaves. Secure a painted filigree contour over the flowers with royal icing, then add more flowers and leaves on either side.

ON TOP TIER, drop a string guideline for garlands on each side of tier. Pipe tube 16 shell borders on top and bottom of tier. Attach garlands of flowers along guideline. Secure ornament on top of cake with icing. Add clusters of flowers at corners of tier. Trim all flowers with tube 65 leaves. Top tier

serves 18, two lower tiers 168 wedding guests.

Decorate the shower cake

Honor the bride-to-be with a cake just as pretty as the bridal cake.

PREPARE TRIMS. Pipe royal icing drop flowers using tubes 35, 190 and 225. Add tube 2 centers, dry. Paint six plastic filigree Swirls with thinned white royal icing and dry. Cut two pairs of pink paper hearts and glue back to back with florists' wire between them. Paint wire with thinned royal icing and dry. Tie each wire with a small ribbon bow. Pipe tube 1 names.

BAKE, FILL AND ICE a 10″ x 4″ round two-layer cake. Place on serving tray. Divide side of cake into sixteenths and mark line at each division. Use a triangle to be sure lines are vertical. Pipe lines with tube 1D. Pipe tube 16 puffs around bottom of cake and add a star between each. Pipe tube 18 top shell border. Attach drop flowers on piped lines.

Secure filigree swirls to top of cake with icing and attach drop flowers between them. Trim all flowers with tube 65 leaves. Insert wired hearts into center of cake. This sweet cake serves dessert-size pieces to 14 guests.

All the dimensional trim on this striking cake was molded of gum paste—and the lovely top ornament with its trio of cherubs was made of gum paste too. Create the ornament and trims well ahead of time. All patterns needed for Pagoda are in the Appendix, starting on page 129.

Make gum paste trims for cake

PREPARE GUM PASTE as directed on page 128. Roll out about 1/16" thick and cut flowers with forget-me-not cutter. Curl petals by pressing from the edge to the center with the round end of a small modeling stick. Dry, then pipe tube 2 stamens. Mount some of the flowers on wire stems for bouquet between pillars (page 14).

MOLD BAROQUE DESIGNS. For base tier, mold eight Classic Shell designs using Baroque gum paste molds and instruction booklet. Tape a 12" round pan on top of a 16" base bevel pan. Dry the shells on the bevel, tops resting on the side of the upper pan. Pipe a tube 5 royal icing spike on back of each shell. (See page 14.)

Mold six Angelica designs for the middle tier. Dry flat. Pipe a tube 5 spike of royal icing on the back of each. Dry thoroughly.

For the top tier, mold six Classic Shell designs and trim off the side extensions. Dry shells around the side of a 6" round pan so the lower part of the design bends outward and rests on flat surface.

Mold twelve festoons from the sides of the Baroque Mantle design for pillar trim and dry on a flat surface.

MAKE CRESCENT GARLANDS for between the pillars. Curve six pieces of florists' wire so they match the curve of the crescent pattern and extend beyond the ends. Cut six crescents, brush surface with egg white and lay wires on top so the ends extend from the points of the crescents. Cut six more crescents and immediately press on top of the first ones. Dry thoroughly.

Make gum paste ornament pieces

PREPARE ORNAMENT BASE. Cut a 4" round base from 1" thick styrofoam. Ice smoothly with royal icing and dry, then paint with thinned royal icing and dry again. Pipe tube 6 beading around the bottom edge, tube 5 beading around the top.

Using Baroque gum paste molds, mold Regalia center shell designs and attach them while wet around the side of the base so the lower part of the design bends outward onto flat surface. Use egg white as glue. Dry. Paint an 8" long, ¼" diameter dowel rod with thinned royal icing. Dry, then criss-cross with ¼" ribbon.

MAKE FIGURES. Mold three gum paste figures in the five-year-old child molds of the Wilton People Mold set. Follow the directions for molding the figures that accompany the molds. Create a different pose for each of the figures. Position the legs so they stand firmly and turn the heads. Attach the arms as directed and dry. Fill all the seams with royal icing and smooth carefully. Pipe the hair with tube 3. Roll out yellow gum paste as thin as possible and cut a sash using the Beautiful Bridal pattern. Attach to one figure with egg white, then repeat for the other two figures. Dry thoroughly. Spray each figure with clear acrylic spray.

PREPARE ORNAMENT TOP. Roll out a strip of gum paste ⅛" thick at one edge and thinned to about 1/16" at the opposite edge. Using pattern, cut roof sections so the top point of the triangle is on the thin area of the gum paste. Cut six and dry on a 10" curve. Roll gum paste to ⅛" thickness and cut top plate using Beautiful Bridal pattern. Dry flat. Mold side extensions of the Classic Shell mold back-to-back and let dry. You will need six.

Decorate the cake

BAKE THE TIERS, a 16" base bevel, a 12" x 4" round, a 9" x 4" hexagon and a 6" x 3" round. Each of the tiers, except the base bevel, is made up of two layers. Fill and ice three upper tiers, ice bevel tier. Assemble the cake on a sturdy 18" cake board. Use dowel construction (page 8), 9" hexagon separator plates and six 7½" Corinthian pillars. Be sure to insert dowel rods into each of the tiers, including bevel and top tiers.

DECORATE BEVEL AND BOTTOM TIER. Pipe tube 9 bulbs around the lower edge of the bevel. Divide the side of the 12" tier into eighths. At each point, drop pairs of tube 2 strings, beginning with the longest pair. Connect the lower ends with a curved string and add dots. Drop three more pairs of strings, each shorter than the last. Pipe tube 7

Continued on page 98

bulbs at base of 12″ tier. Attach Classic Shell designs as pictured, pushing them into the piped bulbs at the base of the 12″ tier. Add a tube 7 top bulb border and edge the lower separator plate with the same tube.

DECORATE MIDDLE TIER. Divide each side of the hexagon tier into thirds. Drop double tube 2 strings from point to point. Pipe tube 6 ball border at base and top of tier, tube 4 beading down the sides. Pipe icing on the back of the Angelica designs and insert spikes into sides of tier.

DECORATE TOP TIER. Pipe tube 6 ball border around base of tier. Using tier below as guide, attach six Classic Shell designs (without the side extensions) on side of tier. Let shell bases rest on top of the middle tier. On top edge, drop triple tube 2 strings. Pipe tube 6 top ball border.

TRIM PILLARS. Insert a small piece of styrofoam into a Classic Vase. Push the stems of wired gum paste forget-me-nots into the styrofoam. Secure the vase between the pillars.

Secure the molded gum paste festoons to the underside of the upper separator plate and to the pillars. Do this by brushing tiny pieces of wet gum paste with egg white and attaching to ends of festoon. Brush wet gum paste again and attach to underside of separator plate and pillar. Dry very thoroughly before continuing.

Bend the ends of the wires on gum paste crescents into hooks. Carefully attach them to the festoons with royal icing. Cover crescents with forget-me-nots, attaching with royal icing.

Assemble the ornament

INSERT RIBBON-WRAPPED DOWEL ROD into the center of the ornament base. Bind ¼″ ribbon into loops with florists' wire. Attach the loops to the top of the dowel rod with a ball of royal icing. Secure flowers around the bottom of the dowel rod with dots of royal icing.

SECURE GUM PASTE CHERUBS' feet to the ornament base with small pieces of wet gum paste and egg white as you did for festoons. Dry. Curve three lengths of florists' wire to create garlands held by cherubs. Leave extra length at each end to attach to hands. Roll out gum paste very thin and using the wires as guides, cut two crescents about ¼″ at the widest point for each wire. Assemble them the same as the crescent garlands between the pillars. Dry, then bend the exposed wires into hooks and secure to hands with royal icing. Attach forget-me-nots to the garlands with royal icing.

Assemble the triangular roof sections on the top plate with lines of royal icing and dry. Trim roof with tube 1 strings and tube 2 beading. Secure the molded Classic Shell side extensions to the roof. Attach the roof to the dowel rod by brushing a large piece of wet gum paste with egg white and inserting it into the roof peak. Brush the piece with more egg white, then center the roof on the top of the dowel rod, pushing the dowel into the wet gum paste. Make sure it is perfectly level, then dry. Spray the ornament thoroughly with clear acrylic spray glaze to protect from moisture.

COMPLETE THE CAKE by securing the ornament to the top tier with icing. To serve, cut the bevel into 34 servings. Complete cake serves 140 guests. The ornament is the bride's keepsake, perhaps to adorn a cake she will bake for the first anniversary.

Rich chocolate icing and hand-modeled marzipan fruit make this groom's cake especially handsome.

MAKE MARZIPAN FRUIT using the recipe on page 127. Divide marzipan into portions, tint, then roll each into a cylinder about ⅞″ in diameter. Cut into 1″ pieces for uniform size, then roll each piece into a ball. Modify ball for individual fruits.

For apples, indent ends slightly with a pointed stick and add a clove stem. For oranges, roll ball on a grater, insert a clove stem. Model pears into teardrop shapes, indent ends and add clove stems. For bananas, roll into a slim, tapered shape and curve ends. Add touches of brown food color. For apricots, press a groove on one side and indent top. Brush all fruits except apricots with syrup glaze for a soft shine.

BAKE AND ASSEMBLE CAKE. Bake 10″ x 4″ square and 10″ x 4″ round, two-layer cakes. Fill layers. Cut oval cake base, 20″ x 10″. (Trace 10″ round pan for curves.) Assemble by centering square cake on base, cutting round cake in half and placing halves on either side of square cake. Place on serving tray. Ice cake with Chocolate Buttercream (page 126). Roll out untinted marzipan thin and cut an 8″ x 4″ oval plaque, tracing a 4″ cookie cutter for the curves. Dry flat, then transfer Beautiful Bridal pattern for monogram. Pipe with tube 4 and over-pipe with tube 2. Center plaque on cake and edge with tube 16 curved shells.

Pipe tube 32 curved shells around base of cake. Divide top edge into twelfths. Drop tube 32 double swags from point to point, then complete top border with tube 16 curved shells. Pipe a heavy line of icing at back of plaque and arrange marzipan fruit. Arrange a mound of marzipan fruit at either end of cake, securing with icing. Attach tube 35 drop flowers with icing and pipe tube 65 leaves. This elegant groom's cake serves 98.

THE COMPLEMENTARY BRIDAL CAKE is on page 101.

Clusters of figure piped fruit are the unique dimensional trim on this bridal cake, designed as a companion to the groom's cake on page 99. This simple piping is quickly done after the other decoration is finished. Delicate pastels give a dainty feminine look—lower tiers are iced in apricot to set off the fruit and the pale yellow top tier.

Decorate Love's Bounty to star at an autumn or late summer wedding reception.

BAKE AND ASSEMBLE THE TIERS. Bake three petal-shaped two-layer tiers—15″ x 4″, 12″ x 4″ and 9″ x 3″. For the base tier bake two layers in 16″ round pans. Fill and ice, then assemble the tiers on a 20″ round, foil-covered cake board using 9″ round separator plates and 5″ Corinthian pillars. Use dowel assembly method as described on page 8.

Before placing the top tier in position, make a hole between each pair of pillars in the top separator plate with a heated nail. Position hole about 1″ in from the edge of the plate. String a 4″ length of ¼″ wide ribbon through the loop on each of four Winged Angels. Insert ribbons through holes in the plate from below and tape ends in place on the plate. Position the separator plate on the pillars, then place the top tier on the separator plate.

PREPARE THE TWO ORNAMENTS. Turn the top plate of a Petite Heart Base upside down to form a bowl, and pipe fruit in it with tubes 12 and 9. Use a steady even pressure and keep tip of tube buried in icing until you have stopped pressure for rounded shapes. This ornament will be secured between the pillars on the lower separator plate.

For the top ornament, glue two 3½″ Wedding Rings to the plate of a Petite Heart base. Glue small plastic doves to the rings. Pipe fruit on the plate, heaping it up in the center. Add tube 66 leaves and dry thoroughly.

DECORATE THE BASE TIER. Divide the side of the tier into twelfths. Pipe a string guideline from point to point, leaving every third section empty. Pipe tube 9 bottom bulb border around tier, then pipe tube 125 double ruffle, following the piped guidelines.

Edge the top of the ruffle with tube 6 beading. Add fleurs-de-lis at the top points of ruffles. Pipe tube 8 top bulb border.

ON THE 15″ PETAL TIER, edge the bottom of the tier with tube 9 bulbs. Drop a string guideline on the side of each petal of the tier, lifting at indentations of the petals. Pipe a tube 125 ruffle and pipe tube 6 top border.

ON THE 12″ PETAL TIER, pipe tube 8 bottom bulb border. Drop a string guideline on the side of each petal of the tier. Following the guidelines, pipe a tube 125 ruffle and edge the top of the ruffle with tube 6 beading. Pipe tube 6 beading around the top edge of the tier.

ON THE TOP TIER, pipe tube 8 bottom bulb border. Drop a string guideline on the side of each petal of the tier and pipe a tube 124 ruffle following the guidelines. Edge the top of the ruffle with tube 5 beading and add a fleur-de-lis at the indentations of the petals. Trim the top edge of the tier with a tube 124 ruffle and tube 5 beading.

PIPE THE FRUIT CLUSTERS. On the base tier pipe tube 12 fruit in cascades between the double ruffles. Use a method similar to that shown on page 10. Pipe zigzag diamond shapes on top of tier extending down side. Now pipe round dots for fruit, keeping tip of tube buried in dot until after you have stopped pressure. Pipe dots one upon the other for full effect. Insert toothpicks as needed to support cluster.

On the 12″ tier, pipe a triangular cluster of fruit with tubes 12 and 9 on each petal. Secure the fruit-filled plate ornament between the pillars with icing and add more fruit on separator plate.

Secure the top ring ornament to the top of the cake and pipe more fruit extending out on the top of the cake. Trim all the piped fruit with tube 66 leaves. If the bride wishes to freeze the 20-serving top tier and save it for the first anniversary, the three lower tiers of Love's Bounty will serve 224 wedding reception guests.

CHAPTER FIVE

Bridal cakes in foreign styles... jewels of the decorator's art

This chapter is an enticing sampler of unique and beautiful cakes decorated in foreign methods. Each cake displays the unmistakable characteristics of the style at its purest. Create them as memorable and strikingly unique centerpieces for formal wedding receptions.

If you would like to know more about these fascinating foreign methods that are the foundation of our own American techniques, study Chapters Four through Nine of *Volume Two, The Wilton Way of Cake Decorating*. Here you will find a complete description of every major foreign method, with many cakes decorated in these styles.

The Continental Method

This elegant method was developed by master chefs all over Europe in the nineteenth century—and is practiced very widely today. In a Continental confection the cake itself comes first, and is a skillful combination of delicious flavors and textures. The dainty decoration indicates and enhances these flavors, and is always completely edible. Each Continental cake is a one-of-a-kind combination of fine baking and delicate trim.

Gâteau Grande Fête

This lucious little masterpiece is a perfect example of the Continental style.

All the continental recipes are in Chapters Seven and Eight of the *Wilton Book of Classic Desserts*, but of course you can use your own tested favorites. Note how the icings and trims echo the flavors of the cake and filling.

A DELICATE ALMOND CAKE was used for the two 9″ layers, with a 9″ layer of crunchy Swiss Broyage sandwiched between them. The almond layers were sprinkled with cognac after baking. Fill the layers with raspberry jam, and refrigerate for a day to mellow the flavors.

ICING ENHANCES THE FLAVORS. Brush the assembled cake with apricot glaze to seal the surface. (Heat one cup of apricot jam to boiling and strain.) Cover the top of the cake smoothly with Continen-

tal Butter Cream, then with almond flavored Poured Fondant (page 127). Let set. Now spread the side thickly with Continental Butter Cream, tinted pink and flavored with raspberry. (Snow-white buttercream, page 126, is acceptable.) Mark the side with a decorating comb.

CREATE THE COMPLEMENTARY TRIM. Using the Beautiful Bridal pattern, pipe the fragile four-part ornament in egg white royal icing. Do lattice with tube 1, outline with tube 2, and when dry, turn over and outline again.

Make a recipe of marzipan (page 127), tint some a delicate green and roll out to ⅛″ thickness. Cut a 5″ circle for base of ornament. Cut out about 36 leaves with the Flower Garden rose leaf cutter and dry in a curved surface. Tint marzipan pink and model six full-blown roses. First mold a cone from ¾″ ball of marzipan. Make three petals by flattening ⅜″ balls into round petal shapes. Thin edges with thumb and forefinger and attach around cone for center of flower. Use egg white for glue. Make five slightly larger petals from ½″ balls and attach to cone below first three petals. Finally make 7 petals from ⅝″ balls. Flatten and furl with thumb and forefinger and attach to cone near the base. Dry, then brush with glaze (page 127).

Set marzipan circle in center of cake and bead edges with tube 3. Using the same tube and thinned Butter Cream, pipe a circle of loops around the marzipan circle. Use tube 4 to finish the top.

Assemble the ornament on the cake by piping a line of royal icing on the marzipan circle and on one vertical side of a lattice piece. Set lattice on line, pipe another line on circle and add second lattice piece. Add third and fourth pieces the same way. Pipe a spire on the ornament with tubes 6, 4 and 1 and add picot edging with tube 1.

To finish, arrange roses and leaves around ornament. This Continental-style confection serves 28 guests with 1″ wedges. Set a rose on the plate of each member of the wedding party.

103

103

This formal and beautiful cake represents the English Over-piped style at its purest. The heart shape is the appropriate motif. Curves are piped and accurately over-piped for a rich dimensional effect. This style demands patience and skill from the decorator, but the resulting creations more than justify the effort.

English cakes in this style are always made of fruitcake. For this cake, bake two 10″ round layers, each 2½″ high, and a third layer in the 14″ base bevel pan. Level tops with a sharp knife.

A perfectly smooth surface is needed for decorating, so follow the steps on the next page to achieve it. Assemble the two 10″ round layers before beginning, filling them with apricot jam or buttercream. Attach 10″ cardboard cake circle to bottom of cake with royal icing.

1. MAKE TWO RECIPES OF MARZIPAN (page 127). Pack any fruit holes or cracks with pieces of marzipan, using a small spatula to level the surface. Dust work surface and rolling pin with confectioners' sugar. Roll out a ball of marzipan into a ⅜″ thick circle, slightly larger than cake diameter. Brush cake top with warm apricot glaze (heat apricot jam to boiling and strain). Place cake upside down on marzipan, then trim excess with a sharp knife.

2. TURN CAKE UPRIGHT and brush sides with warm apricot glaze. Shape half the remaining marzipan into a long narrow roll. Flatten with a rolling pin to a width of about 6″, ⅜″ thick. Using a ruler as a guide, trim one long side so it is straight. Place cake on its side on strip with bottom edge along straight edge of marzipan. Roll cake, patting marzipan in place. Trim seam so the edges butt.

3. TURN CAKE UPRIGHT and trim off excess marzipan around top with a sharp knife. Press seams together with fingers and smooth.

4. PAT CAKE ALL OVER with hands to smooth any irregularities in the covering. Let harden 48 hours so oil in marzipan will not discolor icing.

To COVER BASE BEVEL, brush slanted edge with warm apricot glaze. Shape remaining marzipan into a long narrow roll and flatten with a rolling pin. Cut strip with sharp knife so it is 2½″ wide and about 44″ long—use a ruler as a guide for straight edges. Beginning at one end, loosely roll strip. Lay rolled strip on slanted edge and unroll, patting marzipan into place. The marzipan will extend up onto flat top of bevel. Trim seam so edges butt. Dry 48 hours.

ASSEMBLE BEVEL AND ROUND LAYERS. Cover top of base bevel with buttercream icing or apricot jam on exposed fruitcake only. Place marzipan-covered round cake on top of it, then ice entire cake with a very thin coat of meringue royal icing (recipe on page 126). Let icing dry very thoroughly, then ice again to a perfectly smooth surface. Dry again. Now the cake is ready to be decorated. Assembled cake will stand 6″ high.

PIPE CENTER STAR

PIPE HEART DESIGNS

PIPE FREEHAND SCROLLS

PIPE BASIC STRUCTURE

DO OVER-PIPED STRINGWORK

PIPE LOWER SIDE BORDER

Meringue royal icing is used to pipe all trims. Make about 50 forget-me-nots using tube 101. Pipe five tiny, tear-shaped petals, slightly cupped. Add a tube 1 yellow dot in center. Dry. Transfer Beautiful Bridal pattern to cake top.

Pipe the top trim

Do CENTER STAR. *Remember: when over-piping, complete only two lines of piping before allowing work to dry.* If more than two lines are piped before drying, the work may shift or collapse from weight. While work is drying in one place, do piping on other areas of the cake.

Work from outer edge of star in. Pipe a tube 2 line over pattern line, then pipe a tube 2 line 1/16″ within it. Add a tube 1 line with a fleur-de-lis at the inner points of the star, then a line of tube 1 dots, each 1/16″ from the last line. Go back and over-pipe pattern line with tube 2, then tube 1. Over-pipe the next line in with tube 1. Add tube 1 dots at the points of the star on each line.

PIPE HEART DESIGNS. Pipe zigzag with tube 16, heavy at top curves and tapering down at the point. Over-pipe with straight lines using tubes 15, 5, 3, 2 and 2. Pipe tube 3 ball between scroll extensions within heart. Freehand scrolls outside heart are piped after upper side border.

Pipe upper side border

PIPE BASIC STRUCTURE OF TOP BORDER. First, divide the top edge of the cake into tenths, using hearts on top of cake as a guide. Within each division, drop a shallow curved guideline with tube 3. Fill in between guideline and top of cake with a tube 14 zigzag, increasing pressure at center and tapering off at the divisions. Over-pipe with another tube 14 zigzag the same way. Slightly below this garland, pipe a tube 102 ruffle in a garland shape. Then fill between the first garland and the ruffle with a tube 14 zigzag.

Do OVER-PIPED STRINGS. Frame first zigzag garland with a tube 2 string and over-pipe with tube 2. Just above ruffle garland, drop a tube 2 string and over-pipe with tube 2 twice. Just below ruffle, drop a tube 2 string and over-pipe with tube 1 twice. Below this string, drop a tube 1 string and over-pipe once with the same tube. Add one more string below this with tube 1 and pipe tube 1 dots below it. Top the intersection of each string with a tube 1

dot. Pipe tube 1 balls on cake side below the intersections of the garlands and strings.

PIPE TRIPLE FREEHAND SCROLLS above top border. Begin with a curve piped with a tube 14 zigzag, beginning at edge of cake top and extending in to the top of the heart. Pipe one curve for each side of heart. Pipe middle scroll over the top of the zigzag with tube 5 and over-pipe with tubes 3 and 2. Pipe small inner scroll next, using tube 2 and over-pipe once with the same tube. Pipe long outer scroll last, using tube 5 and over-pipe with tubes 3 and 2. Pipe tube 3 balls between each group of scrolls.

Pipe lower side border

Mark lower side of cake with the same divisions as the upper side, marking them ¾″ above the join between the bevel and the cake. Divide each of the areas between the marks in half and mark 1¼″ above the join of the bevel and the cake. Drop a tube 2 string from point to point, then over-pipe four times with tubes 2, 2, 2 and 1. *Be sure to allow work to dry after piping twice.*

Just above this string, drop a tube 2 string and over-pipe once with tube 1. Drop the third string from the bottom with tube 1, then add tiny scallops above with tube 1. Finish the intersections of all the strings with tube 1 dots.

Decorate the bevel

Using lower side border as a guide, mark ten hearts on the bevel using the Beautiful Bridal pattern. Pipe over pattern line with a tube 16 zigzag and pipe freehand outer scroll with the same tube. Over-pipe the heart and the outer scrolls with straight lines piped with tubes 15, 5, 3, 2 and 2. Pipe inner scrolls with tube 5 and over-pipe with tube 2 twice. Edge the bevel with tube 15 shells.

Add the finishing touches

Attach flowers and artificial silver leaves to the top of the cake and between the hearts on the bevel with royal icing. Your beautiful English cake is complete!

To slice the cake, separate each of the two 10″ layers and the bevel and cut individually. Cut each of the 10″ layers into 1″ wedges. Each layer will serve 30. Cut bevel into 30 wedges. Cut in this manner, the cake will serve 90 wedding guests.

This perfectly proportioned petite cake is a beautiful example of the delicate Australian method. It combines the traditional elements of lace, dainty veil-like curtaining, embroidery, fine tulle work and hand-modeled flowers. All trims are piped in royal icing. Sift the confectioners' sugar three times before making the icing to be sure the icing is free of all lumps.

Prepare trims in advance

MAKE TULLE BUTTERFLY AND EIGHT LEAVES. Tape

Beautiful Bridal leaf patterns to a curved surface and butterfly wing patterns to a stiff, flat surface. Tape wax paper over patterns, then fasten tulle squares over patterns with dots of icing. Pipe the designs on the tulle using tube 000. Dry, then cut around the designs with an embroidery scissors. Attach 4″ lengths of florists' wire to the backs of the leaves with icing dots.

To assemble the butterfly, pipe a tube 10 line of icing about 2″ long for the body. Lay a 6″ length of florists' wire in the icing extending from the body,

then pipe over it with another tube 10 line. While the icing is still wet, insert the wings into the body and prop with cotton balls to dry. Cut the tops from two artificial stamens and insert the thin stems into the head for the antennas.

HAND-MODEL EIGHT GUM PASTE ROSES, following the directions for the marzipan roses on page 102. Add wire stems (see page 14). Cut a 2″ circle from gum paste for plaque and dry. Secure five roses, four leaves and the butterfly to the plaque with icing. Tape remaining roses and leaves into a

bouquet. Add ribbon bow.

PIPE LACE PIECES. Tape pattern to a flat surface, cover with wax paper and pipe with tube 000. You will need about 115, but make extras.

Prepare the tiers

Bake two round fruitcakes, one 6″ x 3″ and one 10″ x 3″. Cover each tier with marzipan, then rolled fondant. Make two recipes of marzipan (page 127). Pack fruit holes and attach cardboard cake circles as described on page 105. Then cover each tier with marzipan. Roll it out to a ⅜″ thick circle, large enough to cover the top and sides of the tier. Fold the marzipan over the rolling pin, place on the edge of the tier and unroll. Gently press into place and smooth with palms of hands. Trim off excess at base of tiers and let harden at least 48 hours.

Make two recipes of rolled fondant (page 127). Brush marzipan covering with apricot glaze (one cup apricot preserves heated to boiling and strained). Coat work surface with non-stick pan release and dust with cornstarch. Roll fondant out to a ¼″ thick circle, large enough to cover the top and sides of tier. Place fondant on tier the same as marzipan and smooth. Trim excess at base.

Cover 9″ and 14″ cake boards with foil. Set the 10″ tier on 14″ board. Set 3″ Grecian pillars on this tier, then center 9″ board on them. Mark position of top of pillars on bottom of 9″ board. Using these marks, glue stud plates to bottom. Remove pillars. Set 6″ tier on this board.

Decorate the cake

MARK PATTERNS. Divide the side of each tier into eighths. Use pattern to mark a triangle at each division, base ¾″ from bottom of tier. Use a pin to make tiny holes in the fondant to transfer patterns. On the 10″ tier, mark the arches framing the triangles. The top of the arch extends 2″ onto the top of the tier, bottom is 1½″ above the base of the tier. Mark the position of the pillars on the 10″ tier by pressing with the stud plates on the 9″ board.

PIPE EMBROIDERY AND BORDERS. Pipe freehand embroidery with tube 000 on the top center of the 10″ tier and within the arches. On the 6″ tier, pipe embroidery on the top edge as pictured. Pipe tube 4 bottom ball borders. Set pillars in position on base tier, insert dowel rods through each down to cake board. Mark tops of pillars on dowels, lift up and clip at marks. Push down to cake board again.

PIPE TUBE 2 EXTENSION WORK on bottom of marked triangles to serve as a base for the curtaining. The first line is piped the full width of the triangle, each succeeding line is shorter. Pipe five lines on the 10″ tier triangles, four lines on the 6″ tier triangles. After piping two lines, allow to dry before proceeding. Pipe two finishing lines the full width of each triangle. Brush surface of these extensions with thinned icing and dry.

PIPE CURTAINING with tube 000, starting in the center of each triangle. Space the lines of icing close enough so no line can be piped between any two. Pipe tiny scallops along the edges.

ADD LACE PIECES. Outline arches with tube 1s beading. Pipe a tiny line of icing on a lace piece and attach on the inside edge of the beading. Continue until all the arches are edged.

ADD FINISHING TOUCHES. Place the 6″ tier on pillars. Secure plaque to the top of the cake with icing. Set the little bouquet on cake board. Base tier provides thirty-one 1″ wedges, top tier twelve 1½″ wedges.

Inventive and unusual construction, heavy sculptural borders and masses of daintily arranged flowers are marks of the Philippine method. Cakes are chiffon or butter recipes, boiled icing is used to cover and trim. Sunrise, a glowing centerpiece, displays this style perfectly.

PREPARE THE SEPARATOR SET. You will need two 7" square plates, four 7½" Corinthian pillars, and four Angel Musicians. Glue the pillars to the center of the smooth side of one plate (projections down). Set them as closely together as possible. Glue angels to pillars and dry.

Set a stud plate in the top of each pillar. Set second plate on pillars, projections up, smooth side down, and mark the positions of the stud plates. Remove stud plates from pillars and glue them to the second plate, using marks as guide.

CREATE TOP ORNAMENT. Using Beautiful Bridal patterns, cut arches from light cardboard. Fold on indicated lines. Brush front of arches very lightly with white glue and sprinkle with edible glitter. Cut the two hexagon bases from 1" thick styrofoam, using patterns. Secure the smaller hexagon on top of the larger with royal icing, then ice complete base smoothly. Dry.

Fill the sides of the top hexagon completely with tube 1 "sotas" and pipe sotas on three front sides of the lower hexagon. Sotas is a cornelli-like Philippine technique done by piping touching curls, V's and C's of icing.

Attach the arches to the three back sides of lower hexagon with icing. Dry thoroughly. Pipe tube 2 beading around the edges of the base and the outer edges of the top arches. Secure Petite Bridal Couple to the base with icing and dry.

PIPE THE DAISIES. Almost all Philippine flowers are piped on wire in royal icing, using a fast assembly-line technique.

Pipe pistils first. Cut about 18 pieces of florists'

wire each about 6" long, twist into a cluster and make a tiny hook on each wire. Spread the wires apart, then insert the hooked ends into a decorating bag fitted with tube 10. Squeeze bag lightly while pulling it away. Repeat until all pistils are piped, then set in a styrofoam block to dry. Untwist the wires to pipe each daisy individually.

Pipe the petals upside down. Hold the wire in your hand and twirl like a flower nail. Dry flowers upside down on a cake rack weighted at one end, with most of it extending beyond the counter. As each flower or step is finished, bend the end of the stem and hook it onto the rack to dry.

Leave tip of pistil exposed and pull out two rows of tube 1 stamens. Dry upside down about one hour, just to stiffen. Add a single row of tube 81 petals and dry. Create a variety of flowers by covering pistils with stamens, using tube 55 for petals, and piping additional rows of petals.

MAKE SAMPAQUITA SPRAYS. Cut fine florists' wire to 9" and 12" lengths. Hold a wire upside down. Start at the tip and pipe three tube 59° petals to form a bud. Pipe more buds at ½" intervals adding more petals as you progress down the wire. Dry upside down. You will need about 60.

ARRANGE FLOWERS THE PHILIPPINE WAY. Loop ribbons and bind with 6" wire. Cut 4" squares of tulle, bunch at the center and bind with wires. Now twist the wired flowers, ribbons and tulle into small bouquets. Combine several of the bouquets and tape the stems together with floral tape. You will need four large sprays for the base tier, two smaller ones for the top tier and a spray made only of sampaquitas for the ornament.

PREPARE THE TWO-LAYER TIERS. Bake, fill and ice 12" x 4" and 6" x 3" square tiers. Set 12" tier on a 16" cake board and 6" tier on 7" prepared separator plate (let exposed projections push into base of tier). Mark patterns on both tiers.

DECORATE BASE TIER. Set prepared separator plate, pillars attached, in center of tier. Push in until level with top of tier. Cover plate with tube 1 sotas and edge with tube 4. Fill pattern areas with sotas, edge with tube 2 beading, and add fleurs-de-lis. Pipe tube 22 comma-shaped shells for bottom border, finishing with tube 16 stars.

SET TOP TIER on pillars and pipe sotas and beading just as you did on base tier. Pipe tube 7 ball border at base, tube 5 border at top.

ATTACH ORNAMENT to top of cake with icing. Push stems of flower sprays into tiers as pictured. The base tier of Sunrise serves 72, the top tier 18.

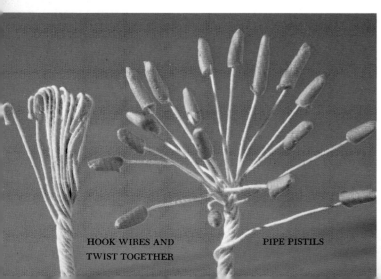

HOOK WIRES AND
TWIST TOGETHER   PIPE PISTILS

CHAPTER SIX

Petite bridal cakes...the decorator's little works of art

Displayed in this chapter is a charming selection of cakes planned for intimate wedding receptions of 100 guests or much fewer. These smaller cakes give a special opportunity to the decorator—while they possess all the importance and symbolism of full size bridal cakes, the decorating will proceed much more quickly.

ROSE WREATH, trimmed with realistic gum paste flowers is truly a miniature masterpiece. See the title page for a close-up view of the wreath.

Create the wreath of flowers

MAKE FIVE ROSES from gum paste using the Flower Garden Cutter Set and following the directions in the instruction booklet that accompanies the cutters. Make leaves as described in the instruction booklet. Tape into clusters of three.

MAKE FIVE ROSEBUDS. Model a small piece of pink gum paste into a cone. Dip the end of a piece of florists' wire into egg white and insert it into the wide end of the cone. Cut a calyx with the calyx cutter. Press edges to make thinner, then brush with egg white. Push wire on cone through calyx and smooth calyx up over cone so some of the pink shows. Model a small ball, brush top with egg white. Push onto wire up to calyx. Dry, then wrap stem with floral tape.

MAKE FOUR DAINTY BESS ROSES. Roll out gum paste 1/16" thick. Using Flower Garden Cutter Set, cut a petal with the medium rose cutter, then roll it as thin as possible. Shape the petal over the thumb, curling back the edges slightly. Make four more petals like this and let all dry a short time before assembling. Pipe a mound of royal icing and insert the petals into it, slightly overlapped. Make five more petals the same way, but roll them smaller. Assemble these in the center of the first petals on a dot of royal icing. Make two more petals the same way, but cut with the small rose cutter. Pipe a dot of royal icing in the center of the flower and insert ar-

tificial stamens at an outward angle. Insert the two small petals into the icing so they are almost straight up. Dry thoroughly.

MAKE FIVE ROSE HIPS. Dip one end of a piece of florists' wire into egg white and insert into a ball of gum paste. Smooth the gum paste down slightly onto the wire. Cut a piece with the calyx cutter, thin the edges, then attach to top of ball with egg white. Bend the points and stipple the center of the calyx with a pin for a natural look. Dry, then wrap stem with floral tape.

MAKE ACACIA FLOWERS. Wrap pieces of florists' wire with floral tape, then twist into sprigs. You will need nine or ten. Roll small balls of yellow gum paste, moisten them on a damp cloth and roll in granulated sugar. Dip the ends of the wire sprigs in egg white and push a ball over each one. Dry.

FORM RING. Roll a piece of gum paste into a long rope about ¼" in diameter. Form it into about a 5" circle by wrapping it around the base of a coffee can. Remove can and dry, then brush with shaved pastels for a shaded effect. Tape all flowers and leaves, except Dainty Bess roses, into a spray.

Decorate the cake

Bake a two-layer 12" x 3½" round cake using a fruitcake or firm pound cake batter and cover with rolled fondant. (See page 109.) Place on serving tray. Pipe tube 1s floral embroidery all over the cake, leaving a 5" circle uncovered in the center. Using Beautiful Bridal pattern, trace couple's initials in center. Pipe the initials using tube 2 and a zigzag motion, then over-pipe twice with tube 1. Pipe tube 5 triple bead border around base of cake. Secure ring to cake with dots of icing, then position the flower spray. Hold in place by bending wires wrapped with floral tape into "U" shapes and inserting them into the cake over the stems. Only a few of these are needed. Attach Dainty Bess roses with dots of royal icing. Serves 68. '

Intricate borders that give a sparkling effect of light and shadow and unusual proportions make Victorian Wreath a very elegant little cake. This pure white beauty will give even a small reception an air of formality.

PREPARE THE TIERS. Bake a 16″ base bevel, a 12″ round single layer and a 12″ top bevel layer for lower tier. For upper tier, bake an 8″ round single layer and an 8″ top bevel layer. Fill the 12″ and 8″ layers. Ice 8″ tier only.

ASSEMBLE THE TIERS. The construction of Victorian Wreath is basically the dowel method shown on page 8.

Ice 12″ top area of 16″ base bevel, lightly press a 10″ cake circle on surface to mark, then insert a circle of ten ¼″ dowel rods within marks, clipping them off level with surface. Set 12″ filled layers on base bevel. Ice this entire tier smoothly and secure to a 20″ foil-covered cake board.

Sharpen a long dowel rod and push through center of lower tier, right down to foil-covered cake board. Clip off level with top.

Attach a 9″ foil-covered board to the top of an 8″ separator plate. Set upper tier on board and press lightly on top of lower tier to mark position of pillars. Set pillars in position on tier. Push a long dowel rod through each pillar right down to cake board. Mark tops of pillars on dowels, lift and clip off ⅞″ below marks. Push dowels back down to cake board. Place top tier on pillars on lower tier.

Decorate Victorian Wreath

DECORATE BASE TIER. Divide side of tier into tenths. At each division on top bevel edge, mark a half-circle with a 2″ cookie cutter. Using tube 16, pipe a 10-petal shell flower in each division. Upper five petals rest on bevel slant, lower five petals on side of cake. Add a feathered scroll beneath flowers, a fleur-de-lis and stars between them using the same tube. Drop swags with tube 13 beneath the scrolls. Pipe scallops on the top of the cake with tube 16, using flowers as guide.

On base bevel, at each division, pipe a tube 16 feathered scroll, then connect the scrolls with two pair of elongated shells. On side of cake, just above bevel, pipe a five-petal half-flower with tube 16. Frame with stars. Add a tube 104 fan and tube 16 rosette within each scroll. Add a tube 18 bottom shell border on edge of bevel.

DIVIDE TOP TIER into tenths. On bevel, mark scroll curve with a 2″ round cookie cutter. Pipe scroll with tube 16. Add a tube 103 ruffled fan and tube 16 rosette at top of scroll. With same tube, pipe a five-petal half-flower below scroll and stars between them. Pipe tube 17 bottom shell border, then add tube 13 swags and fleurs-de-lis above.

Fill a plastic Heart Bowl with Oasis, dampen the Oasis and arrange fresh flowers in the bowl. Place on top of the cake. Victorian Wreath is complete—and beautiful! Top tier serves 30, base tier serves 68 wedding guests.

This frothy petite cake is adorned with a lovely nosegay of red and white roses, the symbol of unity and married love. Arrange bouquets as treasured gifts for the parents of the bride and groom.

MAKE FLOWERS. Pipe roses with tubes 103 and 104 and rosebuds with tube 103. Dry, then mount on wire stems. Pipe tube 66 leaves on wires and dry. Arrange into a nosegay, frame with a lacey doily and tie with a ribbon bow. For bouquets, secure iced half-balls of styrofoam in champagne glasses with royal icing. Insert roses and leaves.

PREPARE AND DECORATE TIERS. Bake 12″ x 4″ and 8″ x 3″ two-layer square tiers. Fill, and assemble on cake board. Beginning with the bottom tier, pipe a tube 32 base shell border and add a tube 13 zigzag around the base of each shell. Mark each side of tier with a 2½″ heart-shaped cutter. Pipe the heart with tube 13 scrolls and add more scrolls and stars with same tube. Pipe tube 16 top border.

ON THE TOP TIER, pipe tube 13 "C"-shaped scrolls at the lower corners on each side. Complete bottom border with tube 16 shells. On sides of tier, mark a curve lightly with a toothpick and pipe "C"-shaped scrolls with tube 13. Add stars with the same tube. Pipe top shell border with tube 16. Figure pipe pink tube 8 hearts as pictured.

Place nosegay on top of cake. Together serves 72 without the 32-serving top tier.

Dainty and delightful, this little cake is trimmed with happy cherubs and love's own flower, the rose. Note the subtle gradations of color in the tiers—deep pink, pale pink and snowy white.

MAKE MANY ROSES with tubes 102 and 103. Make eight tiny roses on a toothpick instead of a flower nail using tubes 101 and 101s. Attach tiny roses to hands of Cherub Card-Holder with icing.

BAKE TIERS in Heart Mini-Tier pans. The two bottom tiers are two layers each, the top a single layer. Fill and ice. Assemble lower tiers on serving tray. Mark top of middle tier for position of pillars and insert pillars as on page 9. Secure top tier to its separator plate, but do not place on pillars.

DECORATE CAKE. On bottom tier, pipe tube 17 bottom shell border. Divide each side of tier into tenths, mark about 1″ below top edge and drop a tube 13 string from point to point. Top the intersections with a fleur-de-lis. Pipe tube 16 top shell border. Attach roses at the sides of the tier.

On middle tier, pipe tube 16 shell borders. Attach roses in a horseshoe shape beginning between the pillars. Attach a Winged Angel at the front of the two lower tiers with icing.

On top tier, pipe shell borders with tube 16. Place on pillars. Secure Cherub and ring with roses. Lower tiers serve 40, top tier serves four.

These pretty cakes are very quick and easy to decorate—yet each is an impressive centerpiece.

Serenade

Sweet peas and airy filigree triangles trim this dainty cake. The unusual construction—an oval tier above a rectangular base—is very effective.

IN ADVANCE, make sweet peas of royal icing as described on page 10, using tubes 103 and 104. Let dry. Paint eight plastic filigree Curved Triangles with thinned white royal icing and dry.

BAKE, FILL AND ICE the tiers—an 11″ x 15″ rectangle and a 9″ oval, each two layers. Place rectangular tier on a foil-covered board 2″ larger than tier all around and center with 10″ round separator plate. Position 5″ Grecian pillars on

plate. Set oval tier on matching plate. Thread lengths of ¼″ ribbon through loops of four 2″ Lacy Bells. Push ends of ribbons into tops of pillars and tape in place. Glue tiny ribbon bows to bells. Set top tier in position on pillars.

BEGIN DECORATING the cake with the bottom tier. Pipe tube 18 base shell border, then, leaving 1″ at each end of side, divide long sides into fifths and short sides into fourths. Pipe tube 16 zigzag garlands from point to point on each side of cake, beginning and ending at the points 1″ in from the corners. Add a tube 17 rosette at the intersections of the garlands. Pipe tube 17 top shell border and edge lower separator plate with the same tube. Pipe shell borders on top tier using tube 17.

ATTACH THE TRIMS. Attach filigree Curved

Triangles to tiers with icing—two on each long side and one on each short side of the rectangular tier, one on each long side of the oval. Secure one cherub from the Musical Trio on cake board, the other two on top separator plate with icing.

SECURE THE FLOWERS with royal icing. Beginning with base tier, attach sweet peas at each corner and on either side of cherub. Cluster flowers on the cake at the tops of the Curved Triangles. On top tier, secure flowers to separator plate around the cherubs and at the tops of the Curved Triangles. Attach more sweet peas on the upper edge of top tier. Base tier serves 77—top tier serves 24.

Cupid's Bower

Simple borders and fast drop flowers create a very elegant cake when the tiers are constructed with this charming separator set.

IN ADVANCE, make many royal icing drop flowers using tubes 190, 225 and 301. Pipe centers with tube 2 and dry. Mount about one-third of flowers on wire stems. When dry, tape stemmed flowers into small clusters. Secure a small piece of styrofoam in Classic Vase with royal icing. Insert stems of clusters into styrofoam to form bouquet. Push a small piece of styrofoam into top of a 5″ Corinthian pillar. Insert stems on clusters into it.

BAKE THE TIERS, 14″ x 4″ and 8″ x 3″ round, two-layer tiers. Fill and ice tiers, then place 14″ tier on serving tray or cake board. Elevate 8″ tier with Corinthian Cupid Separator Set.

BEGIN DECORATING THE CAKE, starting with the bottom tier. Divide side of tier into eighths. At each division, pipe a column with tube 4B and add a tube 16 scroll to either side near the top. Pipe tube 20 shells for bottom border between the columns. Trim base of shells and columns with tube 14 zig-zag. Add tube 18 top shell border and edge lower separator plate with tube 16 shells. Secure flower-filled Classic Vase between the pillars with icing. Attach drop flowers around base of cupids and at the top of each piped column with icing.

ON THE TOP TIER, pipe tube 18 bottom shell border. Divide side of tier into twelfths, then drop tube 14 strings between the divisions. Top the intersections of the strings with a tube 16 rosette. Top border is tube 16 reverse shells. Secure flowers in four small cascades around top edge of tier with icing. (See page 10.) Attach Corinthian Cupid and the flower-filled pillar to top of tier. Secure flowers at base of cupid. Without the top tier, the cake serves 92 guests—top tier serves 30.

119

Fragile flowers add "something blue" to this fluffy, feminine cake. Pipe the bluebells in advance, then just one tube makes fast work of decorating.

PREPARE THE FLOWERS. Pipe bluebells using tube 67 and royal icing. Press foil into a 1¼″ two-piece lily nail. Pipe three pointed petals, then add a petal between each. Add a center dot and push in artificial stamens. Make smaller bluebells with tube 66 and tiny ones with tube 65s.

BAKE ROUND TIERS, a single-layer 12″, a two-layer 8″ and a two-layer 5″, using Mini-Tier pans for the two upper tiers. Fill and ice. Place 12″ tier on a serving tray and center 8″ tier on top. Mark position of pillars with 5″ Mini-Tier plate and insert the pillars into the tier as described on page 9. Secure top tier to 5″ Mini-Tier plate.

DECORATE CAKE with tube 17. Divide side of the 12″ tier and the 8″ tier into fourths, positioning the divisions on the 8″ tier between those of the 12″ tier. At each division pipe a scroll design. Add shell borders. Divide side of top tier into fourths and pipe a fleur-de-lis with a rosette at each division. Add shell borders. Position tier on pillars.

ADD FINISHING TOUCHES. Attach bluebells as shown. Add tube 66 leaves. Secure tiny bluebells in Kneeling Cherub Fountain and position on top of cake. Trim with tube 65 leaves. Single-layer 12″ base tier serves 34, middle two-layer 8″ tier serves 30, a total of 64. Tiny 5″ tier serves eight.

This impressive little cake is one the bride herself may choose to reproduce for an anniversary.

PIPE HEARTS. Tape Beautiful Bridal patterns to stiff board and tape wax paper over. Pipe with tube 2 and egg white royal icing. Over-pipe heart shapes for strength, then add beading. Dry overnight, then turn over and over-pipe and bead again. Dry. Do not add beading to reverse side of full heart. Make 16 half-hearts and one full heart.

Twist stiff florists' wire into a "Y" shape. Paint wire with icing, then pipe a line of icing on lower edge of full heart. Lay arms of "Y" on heart and pipe tube 2 beading around heart shape.

BAKE AND DECORATE TIERS. Bake single-layer 12″ square, two-layer 8″ square and two-layer 5″ round tiers. (Use Mini-Tier pan for 5″ tier.) Ice and assemble on a 16″ cake board. On bottom tier, pipe tube 8 balls around base, then add tube 6 balls.

Edge top and corners with tube 6 balls and add fleur-de-lis. On middle tier, drop tube 2 triple strings. Pipe tube 6 ball borders and fleurs-de-lis. Divide side of top tier into fourths and drop two triple strings with tube 2 between each mark, leaving ¼″ for hearts. Pipe tube 6 ball borders and fleurs-de-lis.

ADD TRIMS. On bottom tier, attach Winged Angels. On middle tier, pipe tube 2 lines of icing on each corner, then position two half-hearts at a 90° angle. Hold until set, then pipe tube 2 beading down center and sides. Attach half-hearts to top tier. Push wire on full heart into cake and set cherub in front. Single-layer base tier serves 36 and middle tier 32, for 68 servings. Top tier gives eight slices.

CHOCOLATE ROSE . . . A PETITE CAKE WITH CONTINENTAL FLAIR

Delicious chocolate roses trim this lavish bridal cake. Pipe them with either Chocolate Canache or Chocolate Buttercream and tube 104. (Recipes pages 126 and 128.) Make 18 and chill.

PREPARE ORNAMENT AND PILLARS. Glue a 4″ Filigree Heart to top plate of Petite Heart Base, then glue a Winged Angel to heart. Glue a Winged Angel to each of four 5″ Corinthian pillars and dry. Paint ornament, pillars and two 8″ round separator plates with thinned royal icing in cream color. Dry.

PREPARE TIERS. Bake 10″ x 4″ square and 6″ x 3″ round, two-layer tiers. Fill and ice smoothly. (Substitute butter for white shortening in Snow-white Buttercream for creamy color.) Assemble cake on a 14″ square, foil-covered board.

DECORATE THE CAKE. On the bottom tier, pipe base border of tube 19 rosettes and edge with tube 67 leaves. Divide sides of tier into fifths. Drop a series of tube 3 strings from point to point. Pipe tube 16 top shell border, then pipe a tube 67 leaf at the intersections of the strings.

On the top tier, pipe base border of tube 17 rosettes and edge with tube 67 leaves. Divide the side of tier into sixths and drop tube 3 strings from point to point. Pipe tube 16 top shell border, then add a tube 67 leaf at the intersections of the strings. Just before serving, position chilled roses on cake on mounds of icing and add tube 68 leaves. Base tier serves 50, top tier an additional 16.

CHAPTER SEVEN

Recipes, cutting charts and other basic information for the decorator

THE BRIDAL CAKE is created especially to delight the bride and groom, so bake it in the couple's favorite flavor. Many decorators use cake mixes, others prefer made-from-scratch recipes.

When you plan to cover the tiers with rolled fondant, be sure to use a firm pound cake, applesauce or fruit cake. A soft cake will not withstand the pressure of smoothing the fondant over the tier.

FILL THE LAYERS with almost any firm filling. Only a few are unsuitable. Any filling made with fresh fruit may soak into the cake and discolor it. Avoid custard fillings, since they must be constantly refrigerated. Buttercream, chocolate or flavored to taste, is popular.

SNOW-WHITE BUTTERCREAM was used to ice most of the cakes in this book, and borders were piped in the same icing. But do not overlook the special effects of satiny boiled icing, lustrous poured fondant or the smooth perfection of rolled fondant.

Most flowers should be piped in royal icing and dried for ease of handling and perfection of detail. Simple flowers for tops of tiers may be piped of buttercream or chocolate canache, then air-dried or frozen before placing them on the cake.

NUMBER OF SERVINGS and cutting charts for various sizes of wedding cake tiers appear on the next pages. Wilton recommends a serving 1″ wide, 2″ deep and two layers high (a height of approximately 4″ for lower tiers, 3″ for small top tier).

THE PICTURE DIRECTLY BELOW shows in actual size the cake serving described above.

This cutting chart for wedding cakes is based on slices 1″ wide, 2″ deep and two layers high. See the preceding page for an actual size picture of a serving of this size. If you want larger servings, such as 2″ wide pieces, the number of servings will be half the number given for each tier. To cut any tiered cake, begin by removing the top tier. Then cut the second tier, third and fourth, removing each tier from the cake before cutting it.

Since almost all brides like to save the top tier and freeze it for the first anniversary celebration, in the cake descriptions we have omitted the number of servings provided by that tier from the total

number of servings. If you plan to cut and serve the top tier to the guests, be sure to add the number of servings it provides to the total servings for an accurate count.

TO CUT A ROUND TIER, move in two inches from the outer edge, cut a circle and cut 1″ wide slices within it. Move in another two inches, cut another circle, and slice into 1″ pieces. Continue until tier is cut.

TO CUT A SQUARE TIER, move in 2″ from the outer edge and cut straight across. Slice into 1″ pieces. Move in another 2″ and slice this section into 1″ pieces. Continue until entire tier is cut.

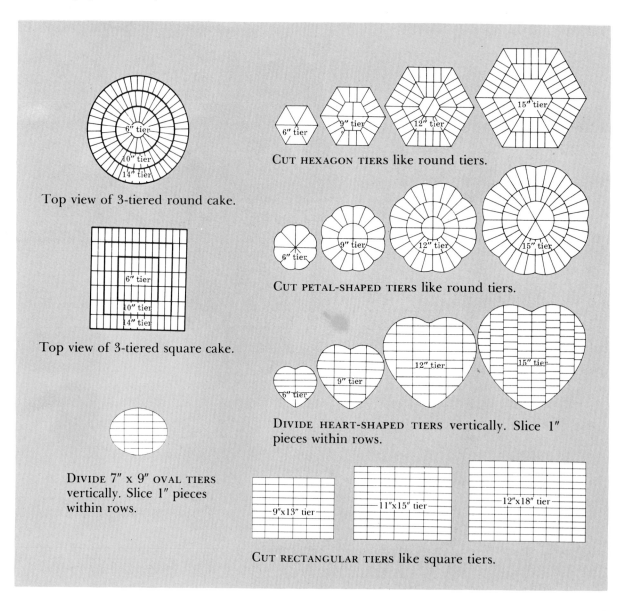

Top view of 3-tiered round cake.

Top view of 3-tiered square cake.

DIVIDE 7″ x 9″ OVAL TIERS vertically. Slice 1″ pieces within rows.

CUT HEXAGON TIERS like round tiers.

CUT PETAL-SHAPED TIERS like round tiers.

DIVIDE HEART-SHAPED TIERS vertically. Slice 1″ pieces within rows.

CUT RECTANGULAR TIERS like square tiers.

Before transporting any cake, be sure it is on a cake board at least 2″ larger than the cake all around. Let it dry for at least half an hour after decorating. If the cake has pillars, remove the tiers above them and also remove the pillars. These will be replaced at the reception. Carve a ½″ depression the exact size of the separator plate or cake board in a large 3″ or 4″ thick piece of soft foam rubber. Place the foam in the back of a station wagon or on the back seat of a car. (You will need a specially-made platform to level it.) Set the tiers carefully in the depressions in the foam. A cake can be safely transported almost any distance by using this method. A stacked cake (one without pillars or separator plates) can be transported using the same method, but without removing any of the tiers.

Remember to protect the cake from dust and from the bleaching effects of the sun while transporting. This is easily done by carefully covering it with pieces of the very lightweight plastic bags used by dry cleaners. Anything heavier will crush icing or trim. Also, keep the cake out of direct sunlight (in a cool spot, if possible) so the heat will not damage it.

Wedding cake serving chart

This serving chart indicates the approximate number of 1″ x 2″ slices that you can expect to serve from each two-layer tier.

SHAPE	SIZE	SERVINGS
ROUND	6″	16
	8″	30
	10″	48
	12″	68
	14″	92
	16″	118
	18″	148
SQUARE	6″	18
	8″	32
	10″	50
	12″	72
	14″	98
	16″	128
	18″	162
HEXAGON	6″	6
	9″	22
	12″	50
	15″	66
PETAL	6″	8
	9″	20
	12″	44
	15″	62
HEART	6″	12
	9″	28
	12″	48
	15″	90
RECTANGLE	9″x13″	54
	11″x15″	77
	12″x18″	108
OVAL	7″x9″	24

Party cake serving chart

Shower cakes are cut into larger pieces than bridal or groom's cakes. These are two-layer dessert-size portions. One-mix cakes serve twelve.

SHAPE	SIZE	SERVINGS
ROUND	6″	6
	8″	10
	10″	14
	12″	22
	14″	36
SQUARE	6″	8
	8″	12
	10″	20
	12″	36
	14″	42
RECTANGLE	9″x13″	24
	11″x15″	35
	12″x18″	54
HEART	6″	6
	9″	12
	12″	24
	15″	35
HEXAGON	6″	6
	9″	12
	12″	20
	15″	48
PETAL	6″	6
	9″	8
	12″	26
	15″	48
OVAL	7″x9″	12

Baking chart for mixes

All baking times are for a preheated 350°F oven. Mixes vary. Cups of batter stated are approximate.

PAN	SIZE	CUPS OF BATTER	MINUTES TO BAKE
ROUND (2″ deep)	6″*	2¼	25-35
	8″	4½	35-45
	10″	6½	40-50
	12″	9	40-50
	14″	12	45-55
	16″	15½	45-55
	18″	18	45-55
SQUARE (2″ deep)	6″	3	25-35
	8″	5	30-40
	10″	8	35-45
	12″	11½	35-45
	14″	15½	35-45
	16″	17½	35-45
	18″	21	35-45
PETAL (2″ deep)	6″	1¾	30-40
	9″	4	35-45
	12″	7½	40-50
	15″	13	40-50
HEART (2″ deep)	6″	2½	25-35
	9″	4	30-40
	12″	9	30-40
	15″	13	40-50
HEXAGON (2″ deep)	6″	1½	25-35
	9″	3½	30-40
	12″	8	35-45
	15″	13	40-50
RECTANGLE (2″ deep)	9″x13″	8½	35-45
	11″x15″	12½	35-45
	12″x18″	16	40-50
BEVEL (Top)	8″	3⅔	35-45
	10″	6	35-45
	12″	8½	40-50
BEVEL (Base)	14″	7½	30-40
	16″	10	30-40
LARGE WONDER MOLD		6	55-65

*For a 6″ layer, 1½″ high, use 1½ cups of batter.

These icing recipes are the ones used to create the cakes in this book. Each has been proven to be both delicious and easy to handle in the decorating bag by repeated tests. For the best results when making a large quantity of icing, we recommend using a heavy-duty mixer such as the KitchenAid K5A or a model with comparable power. A regular electric mixer can be used for smaller amounts of icing, but never attempt to use a hand mixer.

We do not recommend packaged icing mixes for piping flowers and other trims. The recipes given here will give better color and manageability.

To COLOR ICINGS, use liquid food color for pastels. For deep shades, use paste colors, sparingly.

Wilton Snow-white Buttercream

This pure white icing is especially suited for decorating wedding cakes. It covers well, tints to clear and true colors (these will match the hues of royal icing flowers) and pipes clear borders and flowers for the tops of tiers.

    ⅔ cup water
    4 tablespoons meringue powder
    1¼ cups solid white vegetable shortening,
        room temperature
    ¾ teaspoon salt
    ¼ teaspoon butter flavoring
    ½ teaspoon almond flavoring
    ½ teaspoon clear vanilla
    11½ cups sifted confectioners' sugar

Combine water and meringue powder and whip at high speed until peaks form. Add four cups sugar, one cup at a time, beating at low speed after each addition. Alternately add shortening and remainder of sugar. Add salt and flavorings and beat at low speed until smooth. This icing may be stored, well-covered, in the refrigerator for several weeks, then brought to room temperature and rebeaten. Thin with two teaspoons of white corn syrup per cup of icing for leaves and strings. Yield: 8 cups. Recipe may be cut in half or doubled.

Wilton Chocolate Buttercream

This is an excellent, exceptionally good-tasting icing that is easy to use. It is excellent for covering the cake and can be used to pipe edible flowers for the cake top. Flowers can be piped in advance and air-dried or they can be frozen if the weather is warm and humid. Place them on the cake top right from the freezer just before serving.

    ⅓ cup butter
    ⅓ cup solid, white vegetable shortening
    ½ cup cocoa
    ½ cup milk
    1 teaspoon vanilla
    ⅛ teaspoon salt
    1 pound confectioners' sugar, sifted
    5 tablespoons cool milk or cream

Cream butter and shortening together with an electric mixer. Mix together the cocoa and ½ cup of milk and add to creamed mixture. Beat in sugar, one cup at a time, blending well after each addition and scraping sides and bottom of bowl with a spatula frequently. Add the cool milk, vanilla and salt and beat at high speed until it becomes light and fluffy. Keep icing covered with a lid or damp cloth and store in the refrigerator. Bring to room temperature and rebeat to use again. Stiffen with a little confectioners' sugar for piping flowers. Do not thin for making leaves. For a very dark color, add one or two drops of brown food coloring. Yield: 3⅔ cups.

Wilton Royal Icing—Meringue

This is a very durable, hard-drying icing and should not be used for covering the cake. It is excellent for piping precise, long-lasting flowers and for "cementing" sections of trim.

    3 level tablespoons meringue powder
    1 pound confectioners' sugar, sifted
    3½ ounces warm water
    ½ teaspoon cream of tartar

Combine ingredients, mixing slowly, then beat at high speed for seven to ten minutes. Be sure all utensils are completely grease-free or icing will break down and become "soupy." Keep covered with a damp cloth as the icing dries quickly. To restore texture, rebeat. Yield: 3½ cups. Do not double recipe unless using a heavy-duty mixer.

Wilton Royal Icing—Egg White

This icing dries even harder than meringue royal icing. It is used for the same purposes as that icing and also for piping lace, fine stringwork and lattice. It is also excellent for "cementing" dried pieces. Be sure all utensils are completely free of any speck of grease.

    3 egg whites (room temperature)
    1 pound confectioners' sugar, sifted
    ½ teaspoon cream of tartar

Combine ingredients and beat at high speed for seven to ten minutes. Dries quickly—keep covered with a damp cloth. If too stiff to flow easily through fine tubes, thin with a few drops of lemon juice. Rebeating will not restore texture. Yield: 3 cups. Do not double recipe unless using a heavy-duty mixer.

Wilton Boiled Icing—Meringue

This is a pure white icing that is good for piping borders and flowers, but dries too crisp for covering the cake. Grease will break this icing down.

    4 level tablespoons meringue powder
    1 cup warm water
    2 cups granulated sugar
    ¼ teaspoon cream of tartar
    3½ cups sifted confectioners' sugar

Boil granulated sugar, ½ cup water and cream of tartar to 240°F. Brush side of pan with warm water and a pastry brush to keep crystals from forming. Meanwhile, mix meringue powder with ½ cup water, beat seven minutes at high speed. Turn to low speed, add confectioners' sugar, beat four minutes at high speed. Slowly add boiled sugar mixture, beat five minutes at high speed. Keeps a week in the refrigerator, covered with a damp cloth. Rebeat before using again. Yield: 6 cups. Use a heavy-duty mixer if doubling recipe.

Wilton Boiled Icing—Egg White

This snow-white icing is noted for its excellent flavor. It covers the cake very well, but borders are not as clear and detailed as when piped with meringue boiled icing. Do not use for flowers.

    2 cups granulated sugar
    ½ cup water
    ¼ teaspoon cream of tartar
    4 egg whites (room temperature)
    1½ cups confectioners' sugar, measured
        then sifted

Boil granulated sugar, water and cream of tartar to 240°F. Brush sides of pan with warm water to prevent crystals from forming. Brush again halfway through, but do not stir. Meanwhile, whip egg whites seven minutes at high speed. Add boiled sugar mixture slowly, beat three minutes at high speed. Turn to second speed, gradually add confectioners' sugar, beat seven minutes more at high speed. Rebeating will not restore the texture of the icing. Yield: 3½ cups. Do not double the recipe unless using a heavy-duty mixer.

Marzipan

Marzipan is used for hand-modeling flowers, fruit and figures to trim cakes. It is also used as a base covering for cakes decorated with the English, Australian and South African methods.

    1 cup almond paste (8 ounce can)
    2 egg whites, unbeaten
    3 cups confectioners' sugar
    ½ teaspoon vanilla or rum flavor

Knead almond paste by hand in a bowl. Add egg whites and mix well. Continue kneading as you add sugar, one cup at a time, and flavoring, until the marzipan feels like heavy pie dough. Cover with plastic wrap, then place in a tightly covered container in the refrigerator to keep for months.

To tint marzipan, knead in liquid food coloring, one drop at a time, until you reach the shade you desire. To glaze, combine ½ cup corn syrup and one cup of water, heat to boiling and brush on with a small artist's brush. This gives a soft shine. For a high gloss, use just one or two tablespoons water with ½ cup corn syrup. To attach marzipan pieces, brush with egg white and press together.

Rolled Fondant

This is the rolled icing that gives the perfectly smooth decorating surface characteristic of cakes decorated with the Australian method. Rose Wreath on page 112 and Daisy Festival on page 48 are also covered with rolled fondant.

    2 pounds confectioners' sugar, sieved three
        times
    ½ ounce gelatin
    ¼ cup water
    ½ cup glucose
    ¾ ounce glycerine
    2 or 3 drops clear flavoring

Put gelatin and water in a small pan and heat gently until just dissolved. Put sieved sugar in a large bowl and make a well in the center. Add glucose and glycerine to the dissolved gelatin and mix well. Pour mixture into well in sugar and mix with your hands to a dough-like consistency. Transfer to a smooth surface lightly dusted with cornstarch and knead until smooth and pliable. Add flavoring while kneading. If too soft, knead in a little sieved confectioners' sugar. If too stiff, add a few drops of boiling water.

Use immediately or store in an airtight container at room temperature for up to a week. Knead again before rolling out. If storing longer, refrigerate and bring to room temperature before kneading and rolling out. Recipe will cover an 8" x 3" square or a 9" x 3" round cake. See page 109 for covering a cake with rolled fondant.

Wilton Quick Poured Fondant

This icing for covering the cake gives a smooth, shiny finish to the cake surface that is perfect for decorating. See the cakes on pages 74 and 75.

    6 cups confectioners' sugar
    4½ ounces water
    2 tablespoons corn syrup
    1 teaspoon almond flavoring

Combine water and corn syrup. Add to sugar in a saucepan and stir over low heat until well-mixed and heated until lukewarm. Fondant must be thick enough so it won't run off the cake but thin enough to be poured. Stir in flavor and color.

To COVER A CAKE with poured fondant, ice the cake thinly with buttercream. Place the cake on a cooling rack with a pan or cookie sheet beneath it. Pour fondant over the iced cake, flowing from the center and moving out in a circular motion. Fondant that drips onto the sheet can be reheated and poured again. Yields four cups—enough fondant to cover an 8″ cake.

Chocolate Quick Poured Fondant

Follow the recipe for Quick Poured Fondant, but increase the amount of water by 1 ounce. After it is heated, stir in 3 ounces of melted, unsweetened chocolate, then add flavoring. Yields four cups.

Chocolate Canache

This is a delicious mixture for piping perfect chocolate roses. Use for borders, too.

    1 cup German sweet chocolate, cut up
    ⅓ cup whipping cream
    1½ tablespoons confectioners' sugar

First, temper the chocolate. Heat water in the bottom of a 1½ quart double boiler to 175°F. Remove from heat, place the cut up chocolate in the top half of the double boiler. Stir occasionally until melted and at a temperature of 110°F. Remove top pan and cool the chocolate until stiff.

Reheat chocolate to 86°-88°F. Mix cream and sugar together, then stir into chocolate until thoroughly mixed. Mixture will be very soft and "soupy". Place in the refrigerator for about ten minutes. If it sets too hard, allow to come to room temperature and stir well before filling cone for piping. Canache may be kept in the refrigerator for weeks if well covered. When ready to use, bring to room temperature and stir.

Hard Candy

Shining jewels of hard candy add a special sparkle to a wedding cake. See Pink Crystal, page 22.

    2 cups granulated sugar
    ⅔ cup water
    ¼ teaspoon cream of tartar
    Food coloring (by the drop as needed)
    1 teaspoon Hard Candy Flavor

Combine water, sugar and cream of tartar in a saucepan and bring to a boil over high heat, stirring constantly. When it begins to boil, stir in coloring, then insert candy thermometer and stop stirring. Continue cooking over high heat, occasionally dampening the sides of the pan and the thermometer with a wet pastry brush to prevent crystals from forming. It will take 12 to 15 minutes for the candy to cook, but check the thermometer often. When temperature reaches 280°F, turn down to low heat to prevent burning. At this stage, stir in flavoring, as it evaporates if added sooner. When the candy reaches 300°F, remove from heat and pour into greased molds.

Prepare the molds while the candy is cooking. Apply a small amount of vegetable oil in the molds with a small brush, making sure to fill all crevices. Place the molds on foil-lined cookie sheets. When the candy is ready, pour it into the molds, making sure the corners are filled. Let the candy cool about 15 minutes in the refrigerator or until it hardens. To remove, turn molds upside down and pop candy out by pressing the back with the thumbs. Yields about 60 small candies.

Note: Repeat rather than double the recipe. Too big a batch makes the pan too heavy for easy pouring, also the candy tends to solidify before it can all be poured. Do not attempt in humid weather.

Gum paste

Trims made of gum paste add beauty and elegance to a cake that can be achieved in no other way. Baroque trims, flowers that look like fresh-cut blooms and life-like little figures are all achievable with this pliable substance.

    1 tablespoon Gum-tex™ or tragacanth gum
    1 heaping tablespoon glucose
    3 tablespoons warm water
    1 pound confectioners' sugar (or more)

Mix Gum-tex™ and glucose until smooth and dissolved. Add warm water one tablespoon at a time. Stir in small amounts of confectioners' sugar until you can work mixture with your hands. Continue adding small amounts of sugar as you knead until you have added about ¾ pound of sugar.

Gum paste handles best when aged, so store in a plastic bag at least overnight, then break off a piece and work in more sugar until pliable but not sticky. Always keep the gum paste well-covered.

To store for a length of time, place gum paste in a plastic bag and then in a covered container to prevent drying. It will keep several months.

To tint, add color directly to the gum paste by applying a small amount of paste food color with a toothpick. Knead until tint is evenly spread.

Beautiful bridal patterns

All the patterns you need to make any cake in this book are printed here in full size.

To USE THE PATTERNS, trace them accurately on parchment paper. For lace pieces, off-the-cake lattice, or other flat decorating, tape the pattern to a stiff surface (a piece of glass or plexiglass is ideal) tape wax paper smoothly over the pattern, and pipe design. After drying, cut wax paper from surface with sharp knife and turn upside down, with design on a piece of soft foam larger than pattern. Carefully peel off wax paper.

On cakes where pattern must curve around tiers, such as Daisy Festival on page 48, cut out parchment tracing on outline, pin or hold to cake, and trace outline on cake with a pin or a toothpick. Be sure icing has set before doing this.

For other patterns, such as those for the gum paste church on page 83, transfer the tracing accurately to light cardboard and cut out.

Save all patterns, carefully labeled, in an envelope for future use.

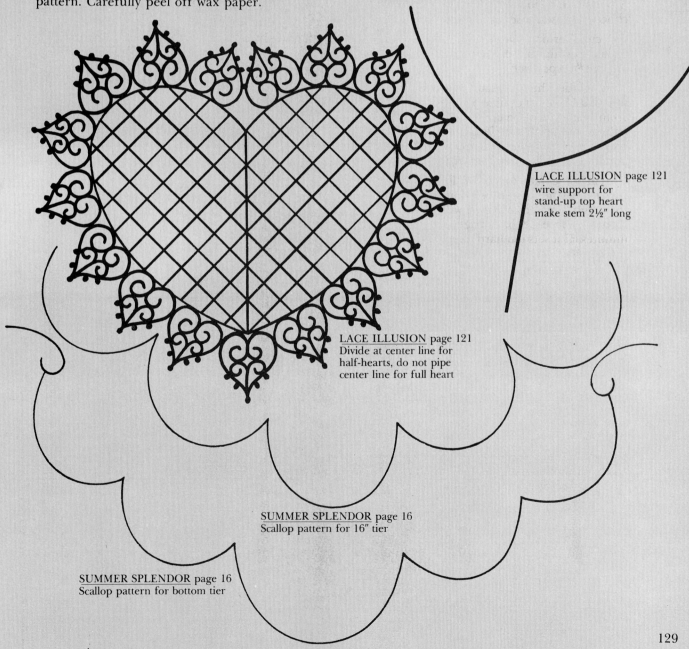

LACE ILLUSION page 121
wire support for
stand-up top heart
make stem 2½" long

LACE ILLUSION page 121
Divide at center line for
half-hearts, do not pipe
center line for full heart

SUMMER SPLENDOR page 16
Scallop pattern for 16" tier

SUMMER SPLENDOR page 16
Scallop pattern for bottom tier

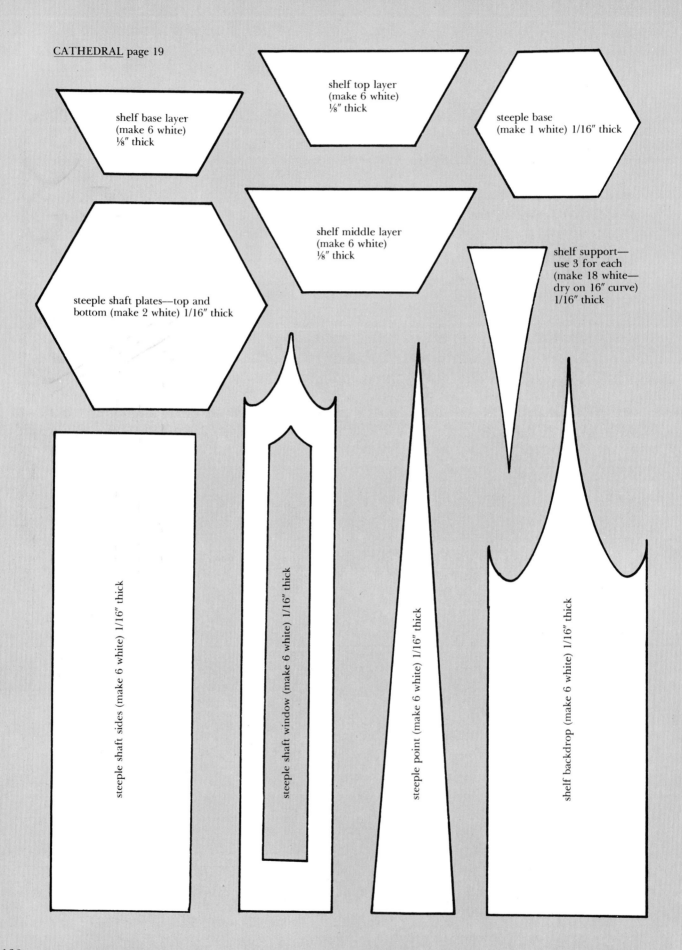

shelf base layer
(make 6 white)
⅛″ thick

shelf top layer
(make 6 white)
⅛″ thick

steeple base
(make 1 white) 1/16″ thick

shelf middle layer
(make 6 white)
⅛″ thick

steeple shaft plates—top and
bottom (make 2 white) 1/16″ thick

shelf support—
use 3 for each
(make 18 white—
dry on 16″ curve)
1/16″ thick

steeple shaft sides (make 6 white) 1/16″ thick

steeple shaft window (make 6 white) 1/16″ thick

steeple point (make 6 white) 1/16″ thick

shelf backdrop (make 6 white) 1/16″ thick

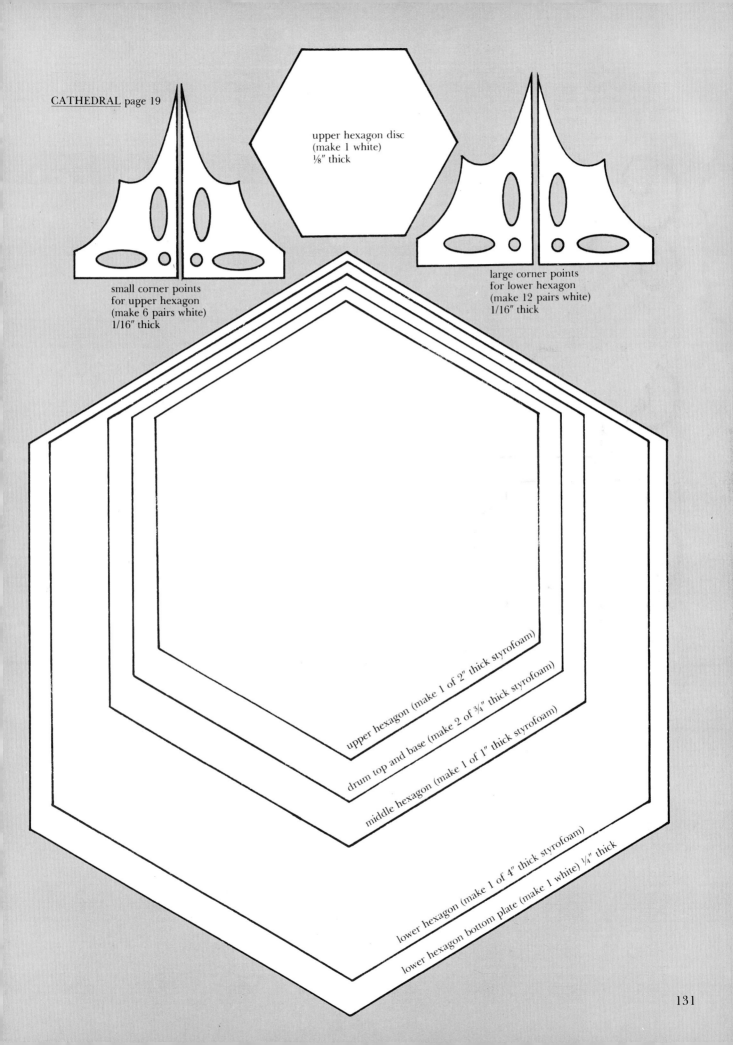

upper hexagon disc
(make 1 white)
⅛″ thick

small corner points
for upper hexagon
(make 6 pairs white)
1/16″ thick

large corner points
for lower hexagon
(make 12 pairs white)
1/16″ thick

upper hexagon (make 1 of 2″ thick styrofoam)

drum top and base (make 2 of ¾″ thick styrofoam)

middle hexagon (make 1 of 1″ thick styrofoam)

lower hexagon (make 1 of 4″ thick styrofoam)

lower hexagon bottom plate (make 1 white) ¼″ thick

gothic design for 12″ tier

drum support—6″ high
(make 1 of styrofoam)

cornice (make 6 white) 1/16″ thick

panel behind shaft window (make 6 green) 1/16″ thick

pedestal
(make 6
white)
1″ thick

piped trefoil design for base tier

inner covers for base and top of drum
(make 1 green, 1 white) 1/16″ thick
cut hole in center with tube 6

inner panel for shelf
backdrop (make 6 green)
1/16″ thick

side walls for upper hexagon
(make 6 white) 1/16″ thick

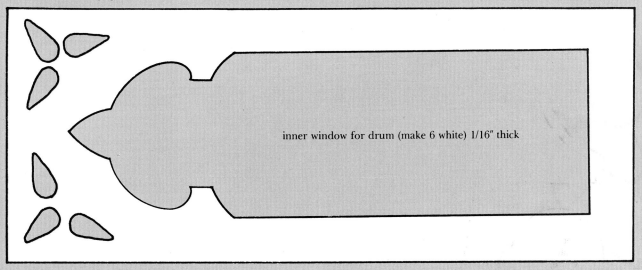

inner window for drum (make 6 white) 1/16″ thick

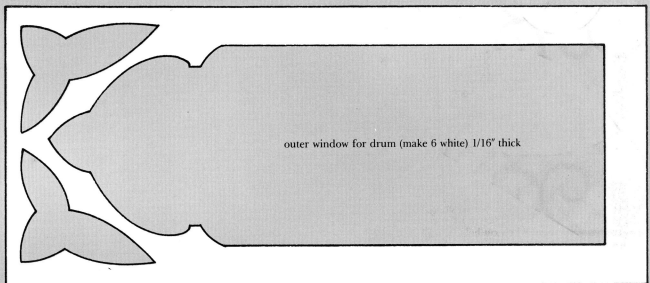

outer window for drum (make 6 white) 1/16″ thick

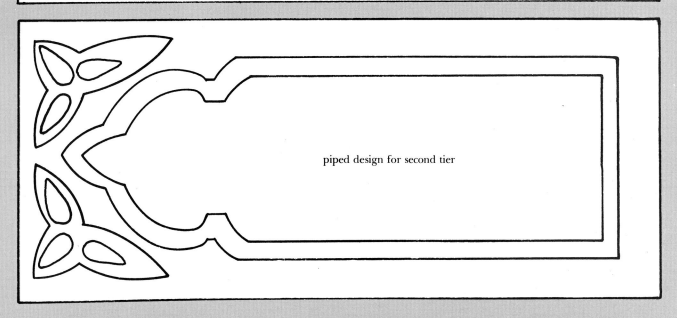

piped design for second tier

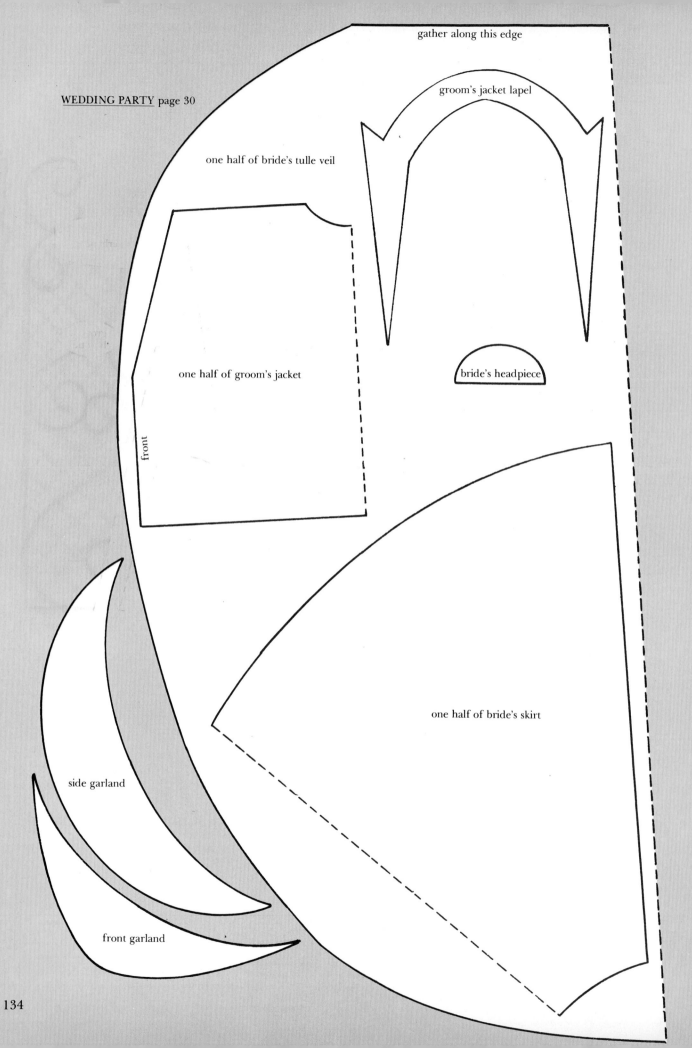

gather along this edge

groom's jacket lapel

one half of bride's tulle veil

one half of groom's jacket

bride's headpiece

front

one half of bride's skirt

side garland

front garland

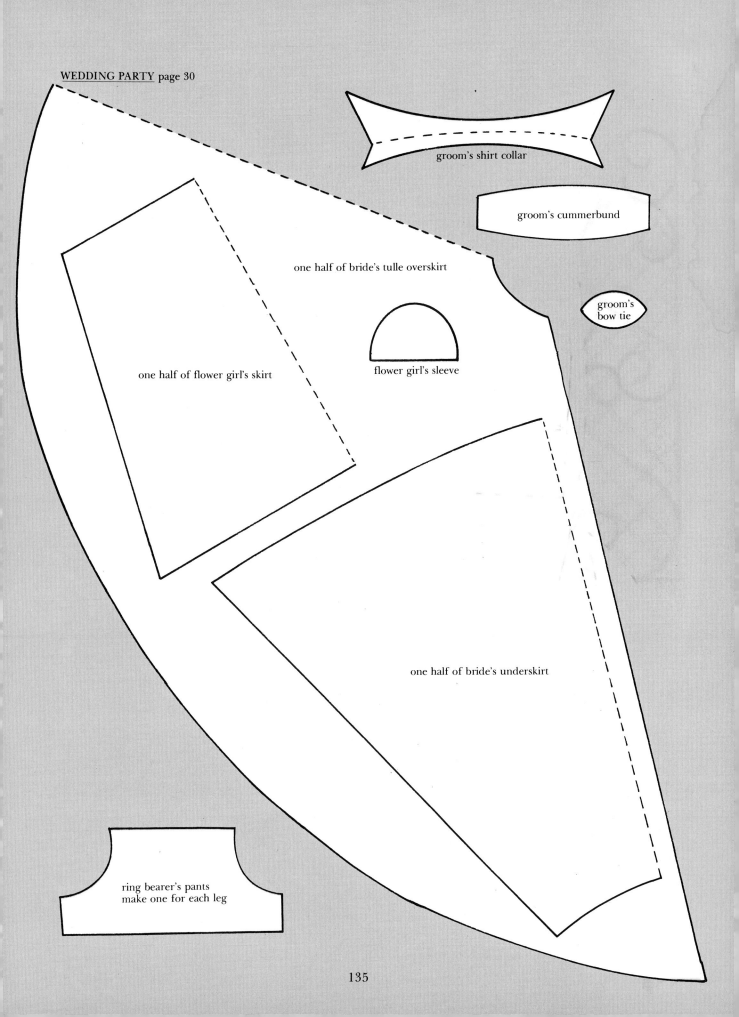

groom's shirt collar

groom's cummerbund

groom's bow tie

one half of bride's tulle overskirt

flower girl's sleeve

one half of flower girl's skirt

one half of bride's underskirt

ring bearer's pants
make one for each leg

WEDDING PARTY page 30
back of groom's pants
(flop for other side)

score on dotted line

WEDDING PARTY page 30
front of groom's pants
(flop for other side)

score on dotted line

DAINTY, LACY SHOWER CAKE page 56
lace pieces

PINK PERFECTION
SHOWER CAKE page 61
one half of parasol top

LOVE'S FANTASY
SHOWER CAKE page 46
one fourth of top design

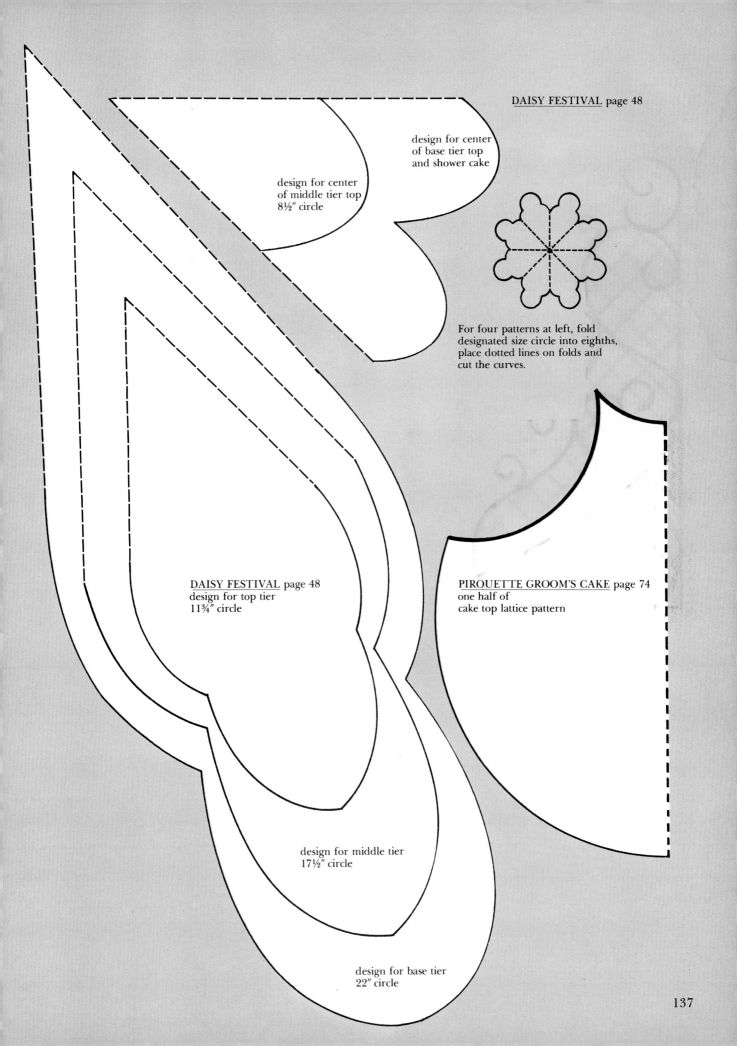

design for center
of base tier top
and shower cake

design for center
of middle tier top
8½" circle

For four patterns at left, fold
designated size circle into eighths,
place dotted lines on folds and
cut the curves.

DAISY FESTIVAL page 48
design for top tier
11¾" circle

PIROUETTE GROOM'S CAKE page 74
one half of
cake top lattice pattern

design for middle tier
17½" circle

design for base tier
22" circle

BLUE MEDALLION page 86
one half of small oval

one half of large oval

one half of top hexagon plate

one half of middle hexagon plate

one half of base hexagon plate

ANTIQUE LACE page 76
pipe on Arch nail

ANTIQUE LACE page 76
pipe on Crescent nail

PIROUETTE page 75
piped top ornament
make 4

ANTIQUE LACE page 76
pipe flat—divide
on center line
for half-hearts

CHRISTMAS GROOM'S CAKE page 69
top and side lattice pattern

ANTIQUE LACE page 76
pipe freehand on both
sides of Large Border nail

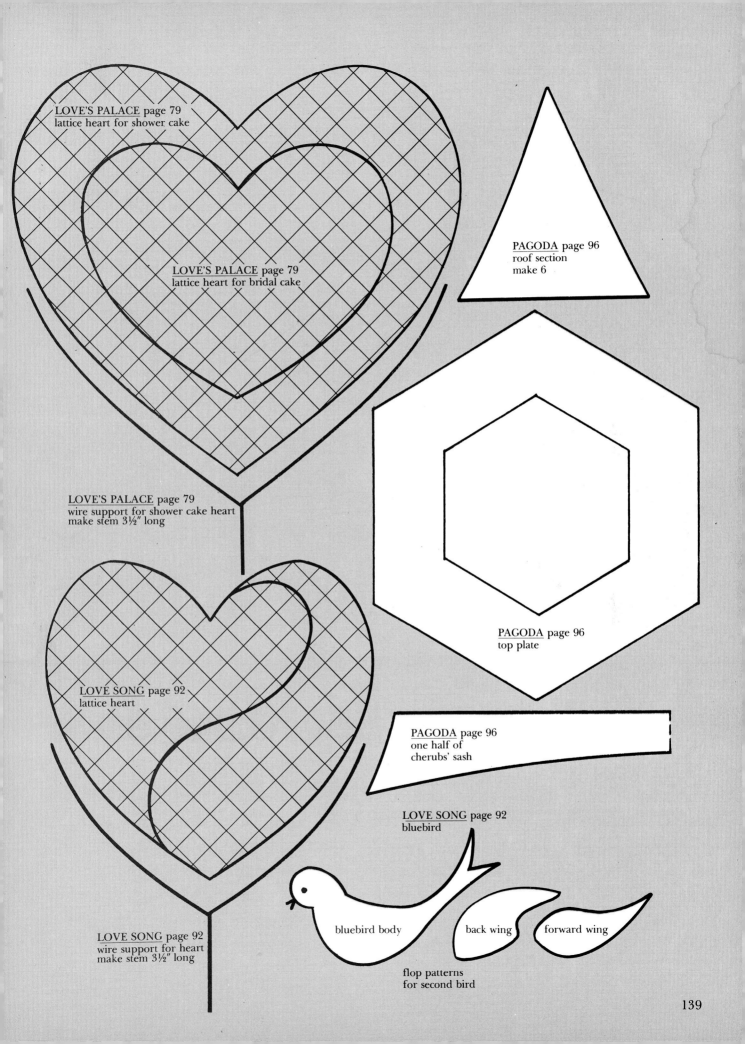

LOVE'S PALACE page 79
lattice heart for shower cake

LOVE'S PALACE page 79
lattice heart for bridal cake

PAGODA page 96
roof section
make 6

LOVE'S PALACE page 79
wire support for shower cake heart
make stem 3½" long

PAGODA page 96
top plate

LOVE SONG page 92
lattice heart

PAGODA page 96
one half of
cherubs' sash

LOVE SONG page 92
bluebird

bluebird body   back wing   forward wing

LOVE SONG page 92
wire support for heart
make stem 3½" long

flop patterns
for second bird

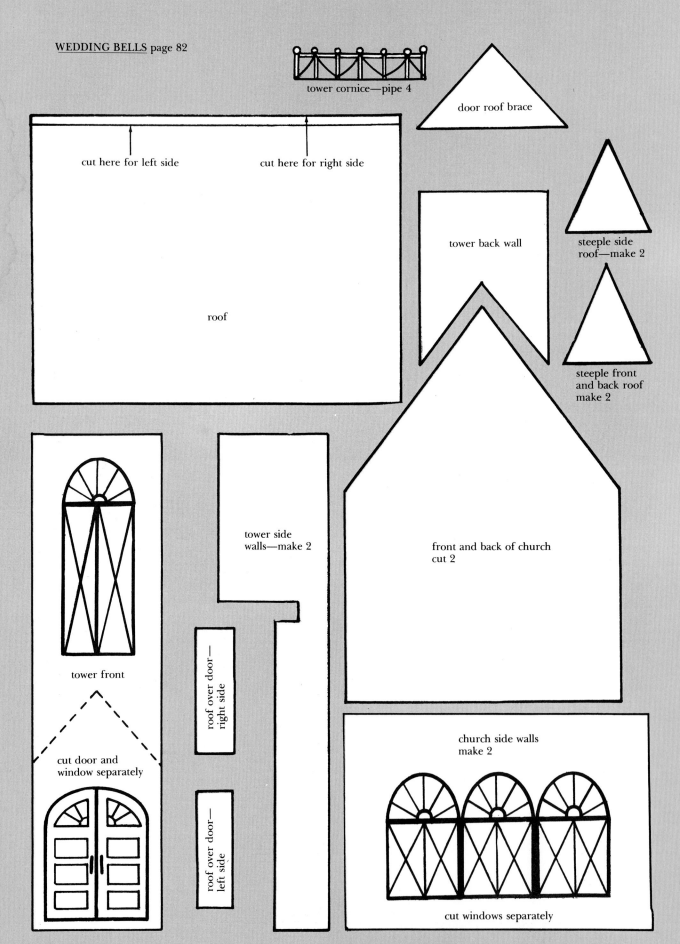

tower cornice—pipe 4

door roof brace

cut here for left side

cut here for right side

roof

tower back wall

steeple side roof—make 2

steeple front and back roof make 2

front and back of church cut 2

tower side walls—make 2

tower front

roof over door— right side

roof over door— left side

cut door and window separately

church side walls make 2

cut windows separately

WEDDING BELLS page 82

1″ thick styrofoam base for church

1″ thick styrofoam base for steeple

steeple sides make 2

steeple front and back—make 2

tower base and step

steeple base

GÂTEAU GRANDE FÊTE page 103
cake top ornament, make 4

use heart for base bevel

ENGLISH OVER-PIPED CAKE page 104
one fourth of cake top

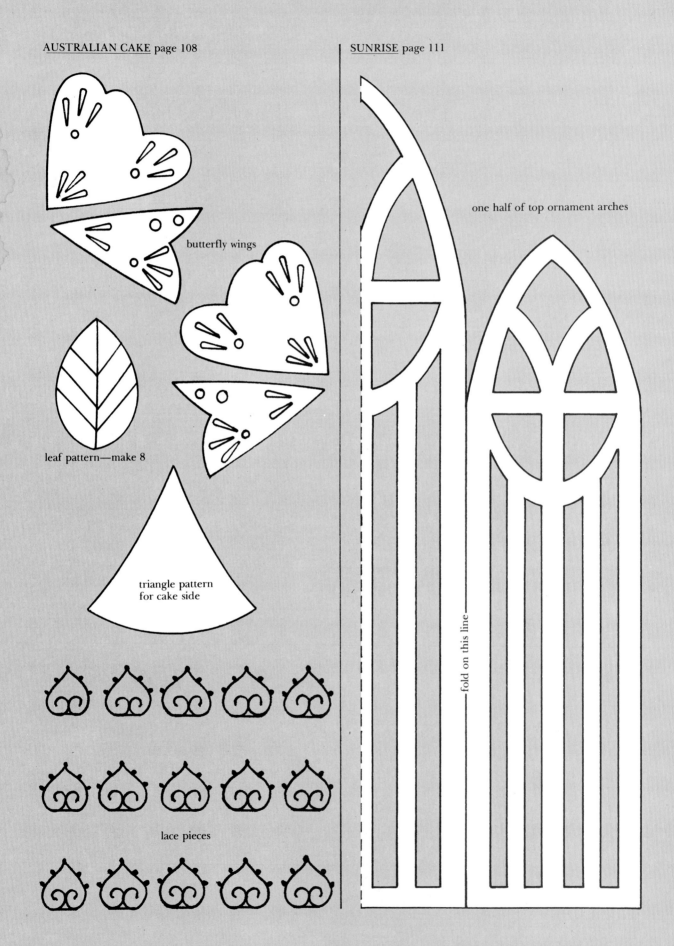

butterfly wings

one half of top ornament arches

leaf pattern—make 8

triangle pattern
for cake side

fold on this line

lace pieces

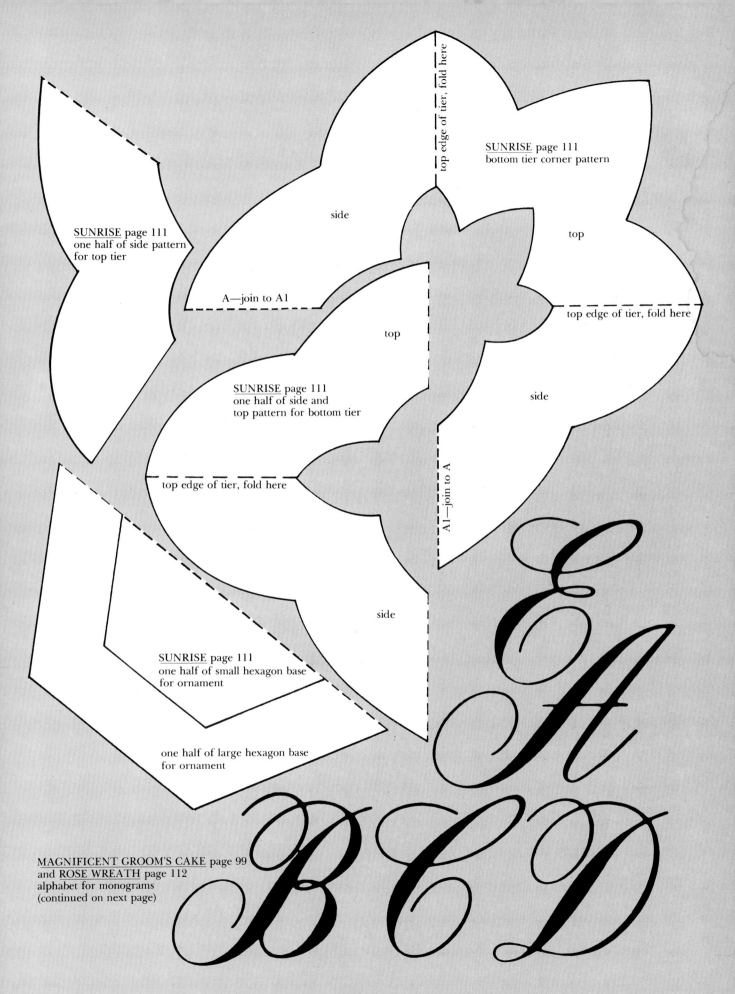

SUNRISE page 111
bottom tier corner pattern

top edge of tier, fold here

side

top

SUNRISE page 111
one half of side pattern
for top tier

A—join to A1

top edge of tier, fold here

top

side

SUNRISE page 111
one half of side and
top pattern for bottom tier

side

A1—join to A

top edge of tier, fold here

SUNRISE page 111
one half of small hexagon base
for ornament

side

one half of large hexagon base
for ornament

MAGNIFICENT GROOM'S CAKE page 99
and ROSE WREATH page 112
alphabet for monograms
(continued on next page)

143

MAGNIFICENT GROOM'S CAKE page 99
and ROSE WREATH page 112
alphabet for monograms (continued)

144